THE VOICE THAT AMAZED AMERICA

THE VOICE
THAT AMAZED AMERICA

The Life, Times, & Singing Career of
Tommy Dix

Second Edition

by
Ken Robichaux

Mount Pleasant, SC

Cover: Tommy Dix superimposed over a photo of Times Square. Cover image created by Ken Robichaux.

Frontispiece: a picture of Tommy Dix from the movie *Best Foot Forward* showing him bursting through the sheet music for "Buckle Down, Winsocki". The image was created by Ken Robichaux using Photoshop.

Photos are from the Photofest Archive, the Library of Congress, and the private collections of Tommy Dix and the author.

Key Light Enterprises, LLC
PO Box 1529
Mount Pleasant, SC 29465

CONTENTS

INTRODUCTION

In the mid–1930s 12–year–old Thomas Paine Brittain Navard (aka: Tommy Dix) began singing on a weekly religious radio show broadcast over WHN in New York City. Going under the name of Bobby Brittain, his appearances would prove to be the beginning of a 15–year career in Show Business and, though he didn't realize it at the time, many of the people and institutions associated with that radio station would eventually have a profound impact on his future career.

The Loew's Theatre Organization owned WHN, and the radio station broadcast from the Loew's State Theatre in the heart of New York City. Loew's also controlled Hollywood's most important movie studio, Metro–Goldwyn–Mayer, and the radio station's call letters would eventually be changed to WMGM.

During this period the station was managed by Edward 'Major' Bowes who debuted the popular radio show *The Amateur Hour* in April 1934, and Ed Sullivan had a weekly Broadway gossip show on the station providing the first radio exposure to many future stars. These people and organizations would all play a vital role in the young Bobby Brittain's professional career in Show Business.

So when Bobby's mother brought him to audition for Dr. Charles St. John, who ran a mission in The Bowery and hosted a radio show every week, she couldn't have known what an important step this would be for her son whose powerful baritone singing voice had developed prematurely. For a while Bobby would be a regular on Dr. St. John's show, *The Bowery Mission Service*, and during this period he would become known to its radio audience — perhaps tongue–in–cheek — as 'Bobby Brittain, the Boy Baritone of The Bowery'.

Bobby Brittain (who changed his name to Tommy Dix when he became a professional entertainer) amazed a nationwide audience at the age of thirteen when he appeared as a singer on *Major Bowes' Amateur Hour* in the mid-1930s. Tommy's unusually rich, deep baritone voice lit up the switchboard and persuaded Major Bowes to immediately invite him back for an encore.

When Tommy was sixteen he appeared before the mother of President Roosevelt during New York City's annual birthday ball for the president at the Waldorf-Astoria Hotel. Tommy sang his own composition about the 'March of Dimes' and then led a large audience in a rendition of "Happy Birthday". The following year he appeared on Broadway where he made the song "Buckle Down, Winsocki" a nationwide pop favorite, and by the time he was nineteen he was starring opposite Lucille Ball in Metro–Goldwyn–Mayer's movie version of the hit Broadway musical *Best Foot Forward*. For the next decade

Tommy performed throughout the United States entertaining a vast audience with his amazing voice.

In 2010, while I was doing research with two friends (John Coles and Mark Tiedje) on one of the actors in the 1943 movie *Best Foot Forward*, John discovered that one of the movie's stars, Tommy Dix, was not only still alive but occasionally performing for charitable events. We immediately contacted Tommy and he was gracious enough to supply some needed information and discuss his memories of working on the movie. That initial contact led to numerous phone conversations between Tommy and myself. We discussed a wide variety of topics ranging from Tommy's life in Show Business to science, politics and many other subjects. Over time it became clear that we shared many interests and opinions, and it didn't take long for us to develop a close friendship. From that friendship sprang Tommy's website (www.tommydix.com), a site that has attracted many of his old fans since it was launched.

This book grew from the original biographical entry I wrote for Tommy's website, but it has been greatly expanded with many more photographs, vintage advertisements, illustrations and additional information. Of course, I could not have assembled the information for this biography without the complete cooperation of Tommy, and I would like to thank him for his time, his treasure–trove of documents, his remarkable memory, his insistence on absolute accuracy and, finally, for his friendship. I hope this book will serve as both an enlightening storehouse of information for his legion of fans, and as an entertaining introduction for those who may not be familiar with this remarkable man.

Although others helped me with this project, I take sole responsibility for any errors in this book. While I have checked and rechecked every date and fact, it is possible that a mistake has crept in. If one is found, though, I hope you will contact me and let me know.

Second Edition

Both Tommy and I have been delighted with the enthusiastic reception his biography has received since it was published two years ago, and this second edition is an expanded version of the first. Additional photographs have been added along with an enormous amount of new information, and a number of errors have been corrected.

Ken Robichaux
October 2014

The first photograph of Thomas Paine Brittain Navard (Tommy Dix)
Taken by 'Offenbach' in the Jumel Building
St. Nicholas Ave. at W. 162nd Street, New York City
(1924)

Chapter 1

CHILDHOOD

Macte Virtute, Sic Itur Ad Astra
(Those who excel, thus reach the stars)
– Motto of the Manhattan School of Music

THE EARLY YEARS:

The winter of 1923/1924 was unseasonably mild in many parts of the northeastern United States because of the unusually warm ocean temperatures in the equatorial Pacific called *El Niño*. In New York City the daytime temperatures during most of December hovered between the 40s and the 60s, and on December 13th the city experienced a record high for that day of 64˚.

On December 6, 1923, as Upper Manhattan's temperature climbed to the high 50s, Thomas Paine Brittain Navard (aka: Bob Navard; aka: Bobby Brittain; aka: Tommy Dix) was born to Anna Navard and Henry Leon Brittain. Anna (age 34) and Henry (age 49) were very much in love, but due to the social conventions, legal sanctions, and mores of the time they were not able to marry. Although Henry visited his son often he was not a daily presence, and the child grew up being raised by his single mother in a poor area of New York City near Harlem.

*   *   *   *   *

Anna Navard, the eldest of five sisters, was born into a Jewish family in Lublin, Poland, on February 27, 1889. In 1892 her family emigrated to New York City where she, her parents, and her sisters lived for the rest of their lives. One day in the early 1920s, when Anna was working as a manicurist in a barbershop, Henry Brittain walked into her life. In those days it took only four weeks of training to become a manicurist, and though the wages were small the tips were often substantial. While Henry got a shave and a haircut Anna brought over her table and began giving him his manicure. As he chatted with this unusually intelligent woman with clear blue eyes and light–brown hair, sparks began to fly and they agreed to meet again. Eventually they fell in love.

Before and during World War I Henry was president of a number of companies including the Birmingham Steel Corporation in Birmingham, Alabama, and the Mobile Shipbuilding Company in Mobile, Alabama. He was also vice–president of the Terry Shipbuilding Corporation in Port Wentworth, Georgia, that was set up during World War I to handle government shipbuilding contracts. He and Edward T. Terry had established their ship building company while working at the offices of the New York construction firm of Terry & Tench Company. After America's entry into the war their company handled government contracts to build steel vessels worth over $10 million.

Even before the United States entered World War I Henry was wealthy enough to

This vintage postcard shows the home of Henry L. Brittain as it looked when he bought it in 1916. He added some rooms and owned "The Castle" until 1924.

purchase an impressive 14–room home in Greenwich, Connecticut. Built on three hillside acres, the Italian Renaissance style building was a faithful reproduction of a 15th century European castle–fortress executed in stone and brick. Henry added several rooms, and though he named his home 'Castle Breatann' (the Scottish word for Britain) everyone referred to it as simply 'The Castle'.

When the war ended in 1918, and his government contracts were suddenly cancelled, Henry branched out into civil engineering specializing in bridge building and heavy construction. But all was not well in the Brittain household.

As Henry's income waned, his expenses continued unabated. He and his wife Gertrude (who came from an aristocratic family and enjoyed playing the part) continued hosting parties, entertaining frequent houseguests, and sponsoring charitable events. Added to this costly lifestyle were the continuing expenses associated with maintaining and staffing such a palatial estate, and in 1922 there were additional expenses when his wife gave birth to a second child. It all undoubtedly put an excessive strain on Henry's income because he was forced to take out mortgages on his property that, by 1924, totaled $115,000.

The financial pressure must have also exacerbated the growing enmity he was feeling in his private life. Shortly after the birth of his daughter it appears that Henry and his wife separated. While she stayed in The Castle, he moved into New York City. But his expenses kept piling up and by April 1924 Henry defaulted on his mortgages and The Castle was sold at auction. Valued at over $400,000, his estate was purchased for just $125,000.

* * * * *

Henry Leon Brittain

When Thomas Paine Brittain Navard was born there were no wars being waged that occupied the attention of the Western World, and there were not even any perceived threats of war. The world was at peace and the American economy was strong and growing.

Anna Navard was a smart, determined, proud, demanding woman who refused to accept Public Assistance no matter how dire their financial situation. Moving from rented apartment to rented apartment, Anna supported her son by buying and selling knickknacks, furniture, and other items she found at the auctions and estate sales advertised every Thursday in the *New York World–Telegram*. Sometimes she rented more than one apartment, sub–leasing the extra one for a bit more money than she was paying. Occasionally, when their apartment was large enough, she rented out one of her 'extra' rooms to another single mother and her child. She also continued to work as a manicurist when she could. Their apartments, usually located on the edge of Harlem, were sometimes cold–water flats with communal toilets shared by a number of families.

None of this was new for Anna. Occasionally advertising in the 'Want Ads' of the newspaper under FURNITURE FOR SALE, she had been supporting herself in enterprising ways even before her son was born. It was a difficult, stressful, daily scramble that was not always very rewarding, but it allowed her to be free and independent.

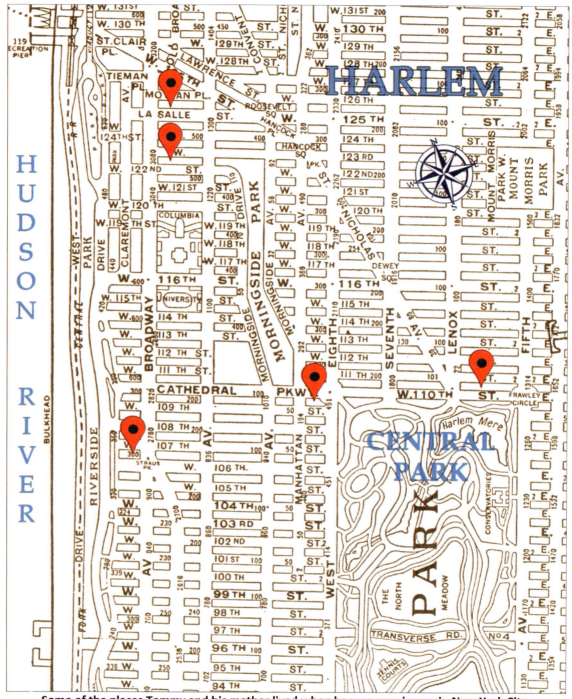

Some of the places Tommy and his mother lived when he was growing up in New York City
(This is a 1937 map of Manhattan's Upper West Side)

Anna thought of another way to make some money when Jimmy Walker, New York City's flamboyant mayor, organized a "Beer for Taxation" parade urging the repeal of Prohibition so the city could once again impose a tax on beer. Generally called the "We Want Beer" parade, this was a massive spectacle held on May 14, 1932. A crowd of over a half million watched as Mayor Walker led 70 bands, 50 floats, and almost 100,000 marchers down 5th Avenue and over to Central Park West.

Anna saw this event as a grand opportunity. She purchased a stack of colorful pamphlets that were titled *Beer* for five cents each and went through the crowd of spectators with her eight–year–old son selling them for ten cents each. Once again her initiative and resourcefulness paid off as they quickly sold all of their pamphlets.

Tommy's mother was a great admirer of both Thomas Paine, one of America's Founding Fathers, and of Robert G. Ingersoll, the 19th century orator and advocate of free thought, humanism and agnosticism. Because of her admiration of Ingersoll she called her son "Bob" or "Bobby", and it was by the name Bob Navard that the future Tommy Dix would be known during much of his childhood.

Trivia:
- Tommy's maternal grandfather, Isidor (or Isidore), was a Jewish cantor before he came to America. His wife's name was Rebecca Ruth "Rose".
- Tommy's paternal grandfather, the Reverend James L. Brittain, was a Methodist minister in Birmingham, Alabama.
- Tommy was related to Chief Justice John Marshall, the longest serving Supreme Court Chief Justice in U.S. history.
- Tommy's father died on August 14, 1959. According to his obituary in *The New York Times*, "*Mr. Brittain had the refreshment and soft–drink concession in 1898 at the World's Fair in St. Louis. On opening day he saw an Armenian food vendor at an adjoining stand baking small, sweet pancakes on a griddle. The griddle was cold and the dough curled in the form of cones. Mr. Brittain picked up the curled cakes, inverted them over scoops of ice cream, and sold them to some girls who were standing nearby. Thus the ice cream cone was born.*"
- Anna's surname in Poland may have been Newert (or, perhaps, Neuwert or Neuwirth). Her family's surname was apparently changed to 'Navard' when they came to the United States.
- Anna became a naturalized citizen of the United States on July 27th, 1934.
- Anna Navard lived to be 90. She died in a nursing home in The Bronx in April 1979.

CELIAC DISEASE:

Beginning around the age of three little Bobby began having a number of medical problems and exhibiting many of the symptoms of starvation — swelling of the abdomen, stunted growth, fatigue, diarrhea, cramps, and anemia. It would not be until Bobby was seven that he was correctly diagnosed as having Celiac Disease, an autoimmune digestive disease that interferes with the absorption of nutrients from food. People who suffer from Celiac Disease are unable to properly digest fats and wheat protein (gluten), and they have to adhere to a very strict diet.

Once his medical problem was properly diagnosed and treated Bobby began to grow normally, but time had been lost and he would grow to be no taller than 5 feet 4 inches (according to his army records). It may be possible that the Celiac Disease allowed his diaphragm to enlarge which, in turn, allowed him to develop an unusually powerful singing

Bobby Brittain (Tommy Dix)
(c. 1930)

voice. True or not, singing would quickly become an important part of Bobby's life. While performing with the Trinity Church choir his voice dropped from an alto to a baritone and Bobby began to amaze people with the unexpected maturity of his singing voice.

But though his voice had grown and matured beyond his years, Bobby's body had not. Throughout his childhood little Bobby Navard would always be aware of, and sometimes disheartened by the fact that he wasn't as tall as others his age.

Trivia:
– According to the University of Chicago's Celiac Disease Center, Celiac Disease affects 1% of healthy, average Americans. But 97% of them are undiagnosed.

EPIPHANY:

By the mid–1930s Prohibition had ended but the country was still in the grip of The Great Depression. Although unemployment in the United States had fallen from its high of 25% to around 17%, many people were working only part–time and many others had dropped out of the workforce. Times were tough for much of the population and people were drawn to cheap entertainment that could help them forget their troubles.

To satisfy that need radio shows became very popular. As radio technology improved, the radio sets themselves became cheaper and cheaper, dropping in price from $140 or more in 1929 to $45 or less in 1933. Everyone, it seemed, wanted one. It was free entertainment and there were shows that appealed to every taste. By 1935 22 million American households owned a radio, including most families that lived in urban areas.

But while many families were listening to shows like *Amos 'n' Andy*, *Gang Busters*, Fred Allen's *Town Hall Tonight*, and Jack Benny's *The Jell–O Program*, Bobby's mother insisted that their radio be tuned to only cultural and educational programs like *Lowell Thomas*, *The March of Time*, and *The New York Metropolitan Opera*. There were a few exceptions, however, and one of them was the popular children's show *Uncle Don*.

Don Carney, who broadcast from WOR in New York City from 1928 to 1947, was known to a huge audience of children as simply "Uncle Don". Airing at 5 PM six nights a week, Monday through Saturday, his half hour program was a combination of original stories and songs, jokes, advice, personal messages, birthday announcements, club news, and lots of commercials for such products as Maltrex cereal, Bosco chocolate syrup, Lionel electric trains, and Borden's dairy products to name but a few. It is estimated that up to five million children in seven states listened to him every evening as he opened his program with the familiar phrase, "Hello, girls and boys, this is your Uncle Don." Bobby Navard was one of those children.

> **Trivia:**
> – Don Carney's real name was Howard Rice (1897–1954).
> – It's a frequently told story that one evening, when he didn't realize his show's microphone had been inadvertently left on, Uncle Don muttered *"There! That ought to hold the little bastards."* The story is not true.

Movies provided another form of cheap entertainment. Hollywood in general, and movie theaters in particular, were hit hard by The Depression at the beginning of the decade. Four thousand movie theaters closed between 1930 and 1932, and by 1933 the RKO, Paramount, and Universal movie studios were in receivership. As attendance slumped the cost of going to a movie dropped from an average of 35 cents in 1929 to less than 25 cents in 1935, and theaters were giving away prizes and showing double features to attract audiences.

But by the mid–1930s the popularity of motion pictures had rebounded. The Hollywood studios had reorganized and adjusted to the changing tastes of the public, and the technology of "talking pictures" had matured and created new captivating stars. Musicals, a genre that had gone into decline in the early 1930s, now made a comeback with multi–talented stars like Maurice Chevalier, James Cagney, Fred Astaire, Dick Powell, Shirley Temple, Ruby Keeler, and Ginger Rogers appearing in such movies as *42nd Street*, *The Merry Widow*, *Footlight Parade*, *Top Hat,* and *Curly Top*. Two of these new stars who attracted an avid following were Jeanette MacDonald and Nelson Eddy. Coming together almost by accident, their on–screen chemistry ignited a generation of movie goers as they sang their way through eight films together.

Bobby went to the movies as often as possible with his mother and/or his father. Although his mother preferred travelogues, documentaries like *Africa Speaks* ("*Thrilling Adventure in the Unexplored Regions of Equatorial Africa*"), and any movie starring Paul Robeson whose political convictions she shared, she also took her son to other movies that she felt were *important*. Bobby's father, on the other hand, often took him to see movies like *The Bride of Frankenstein* and Alfred Hitchcock's suspense thriller *The 39 Steps*.

The mid–to–late 1930s were a wonderful time to go to a movie. Strictly enforced censorship provided a wide variety of films that the whole family could watch, and in addition to their usual lineup of comedies, dramas, horror films, mysteries, crime and gangster movies, adaptations of popular plays, costume adventures, westerns and musicals, every major studio spent time and money adding prestige pictures to their lineup that were usually based on important literary sources or historic events. For example, *Mutiny on the Bounty*, *The Crusades*, *Les Misérables*, *David Copperfield*, *Anna Karenina*, and *A Midsummer Night's Dream* were all released by Hollywood in 1935.

Little Bobby Navard's epiphany came unexpectedly one day when his mother brought him to see Nelson Eddy and Jeanette MacDonald's first film, *Naughty Marietta*. Set in the New Orleans of Louis XV, and featuring pirates, Louisiana bayous, and frontiersmen dressed in fringed jackets and coonskin hats, this romantic M–G–M operetta was voted one of the 'Ten Best Pictures of 1935' by the New York film critics and received an Oscar nomination for 'Best Picture'.

In the darkened theater, when Bobby heard Nelson Eddy sing "Ah, Sweet Mystery of Life" with Jeanette MacDonald, tears began rolling down his cheeks. Suddenly, like being hit with the proverbial 'bolt of lightning', he knew beyond any doubt that he wanted to sing like that for the rest of his life. After the movie was over he excitedly told his mother of his unexpected but heartfelt conviction, but she was skeptical. She knew

how difficult it was to make a living as a singer and she didn't support his decision. She didn't support it, that is, until one day when Bobby asked to participate in a local Thanksgiving tradition where children raised money by performing on the sidewalks in their neighborhood.

Bobby's idea was unusual. Instead of performing on the sidewalk he wanted to sing for the customers in a nearby saloon. As might be expected Bobby's mother was reluctant at first, but she eventually gave in. While she waited outside, little Bobby went into the saloon and sang a popular Fred Astaire number, "Cheek to Cheek". He was an immediate hit with the patrons, and he followed–up by singing a number of requests beginning with "When Irish Eyes Are Smiling". When he finished he walked out and handed his mother almost $5, close to a week's income for her. Bobby's mother couldn't believe her eyes. Hesitantly, perhaps, but certainly with renewed confidence, she suggested that he try singing in another saloon.

It was now clear to Bobby's mother that he was going to sing whenever and wherever he could. Surrendering to the inevitable, she decided he needed a 'professional' name so, using the first name by which he was known to everyone and his father's last name, she gave him the name Bobby Brittain. Now, whenever Bobby sang for people he would no longer be Thomas Navard or Bobby Navard, he would be known as Bobby Brittain.

Chapter 2

THE BOY BARITONE

***THE BOWERY MISSION SERVICE* RADIO SHOW:**

Changing from skeptic to promoter, Anna began seeking out new singing opportunities for her son. She heard that the leader of a religious mission in The Bowery, Dr. Charles St. John, had a weekly radio program broadcast from the mission every week over WHN. Along with its inspirational content, the program also featured singers and musicians. Although the performers were not paid, *The Bowery Mission Service's* popular hour–long show was heard in six states and provided valuable local exposure. After auditioning, Bobby was not only accepted for the program, he became a regular who was sometimes referred to (perhaps jokingly) by the euphonious appellation 'Bobby Brittain, the Boy Baritone of The Bowery'.

Charles J. St. John
Superintendent of The Bowery Mission

Located in the southern part of Manhattan, The Bowery in the 1930s was a squalid, polluted area that became the final destination for alcoholics, the homeless and the hopeless. Just fifteen blocks long, this was the 'skid row' of New York City that featured flop–houses, hockshops, second–hand clothing stores, and more saloons per block than anywhere else in the country. Often called 'The Last Mile', 'The Meanest Mile', 'Dead End', and 'The Street of Forgotten Men', this is where the 'Bowery Bums' panhandled for nickels or stole whatever they could for their next drink of cheap alcohol in one of the area's many filthy saloons.

Not all of these human derelicts had been idle ne'er–do–wells or thieves or social outcasts, however. Many had once been successful businessmen, artists, skilled laborers, lawyers, doctors, and even ministers. But uncontrollable addictions, or the inability to deal with the pressures of daily life, had driven them to destroy their lives and the lives of those they loved. If you were a person who had hit bottom, The Bowery was where you went to die.

One ray of hope in The Bowery came from The Bowery Mission. Established in 1879 it was, for many men, a last ray of hope. When anyone came to The Bowery Mission they were given a cup of coffee, some food, a bath, and a place to sleep. The next morning, if they wanted to stay and accept help, their clothes were deloused and, if necessary, replaced. If their clothes could be repaired the person was shown how to repair them. Then they were given a razor so they could shave, a free haircut, and a meal. Once the person

Tommy & his mother Anna Navard (mid–1930s)

felt more human he was assisted in either finding a job or returning home. In 1939, for instance, the Mission sent home an average of one man a day. Over time sixteen thousand jobs were found for those who wanted to rejoin society. Spiritual guidance was also available for those who wanted it, but no one was forced to accept Christianity.

The Bowery Mission's outreach programs were financed by proceeds from *The Christian Herald* magazine, donations from the public and other religious organizations, and in the late 1930s from *The Bowery Mission Service* radio program. Interspersed among the show's homilies and musical interludes, the superintendent of The Bowery Mission, Dr. Charles St. John (who was known as 'Doc' to The Bowery and 'Charlie' to his friends), would put some of the residents of the Mission on the air to give their backgrounds, former occupations, and ask for jobs. The Mission received an average of four job offers each broadcast. Dr. St. John would also ask for anything that was needed: clothes, furniture, wheelchairs, small radios, false teeth, coal, and even cemetery plots. When a plea was made for something that the Mission's destitute community required, it was almost always answered quickly by someone in the show's listening audience.

After Bobby was accepted for the show his mother would take him on the long journey from the Upper West Side down to The Bowery where his strong baritone singing voice could boom across the airways. After the show was over Anna would take her son a little further southeast to the impoverished Jewish neighborhood where they would dine at well known places like Katz's Delicatessen on traditional Jewish dishes like matzo–ball soup, cheese blintzes, and sour milk.

THE HIGH SCHOOL OF MUSIC & ART:

In 1936, when Bobby graduated from his elementary school at PS165, a new and unique opportunity presented itself. The mayor of New York City, Fiorello H. LaGuardia, had just authorized the establishment of a high school designed to provide training in the visual and performing arts for promising students. New students were chosen through auditions or appraisals, and Bobby jumped at the chance to attend.

The High School of Music and Art was a pet project of Mayor LaGuardia who felt that music and art were essential ingredients for a full, happy life. However, separating talented youngsters from other students, and giving them a unique opportunity to develop their musical and artistic skills, was a controversial plan for a public educational institution at that time, and it took all of the mayor's influence to create and establish the new school.

Fiorello H. LaGuardia (1937)
Mayor of New York City 1934–1945

The high school was open to any New York City student between the ages of twelve and fourteen no matter what their ethnicity, socioeconomic background, or where in the city they lived. But to attend, an applicant had to go through a rigorous evaluation that assessed both their musical or artistic aptitude, and their facility for understanding the basic elements of their discipline (such as sensitivity to musical sound). In the end, though, it was primarily through the applicant's musical performance or art portfolio that they were judged. Since the appraisal was largely subjective, the examiners worked in pairs.

This was not meant to be a school that trained aspiring professional musicians and artists, although many of them did go on to find great success in those fields, but rather a school that allowed students with an aptitude for music or art to fully understand their special gift and thereby enrich their lives and the lives of those around them. An article in *The New York Times* clarified the purpose of the school when it stated:

> **. . . the city's first school exclusively for gifted children [will not have] a vocational function, nor does it propose to offer specialized training that will lead directly to employment upon graduation . . . [but] will build a sound base for later specialization and will give preparation to those who wish to continue their studies in higher educational institutions.**

The first class of 250 pupils (125 in music and 125 in art) assembled at the beginning of 1936 in the former New York Training School for Teachers. Prominently situated on a ridge overlooking St. Nicholas Park, this gothic structure of limestone and brick was located on the edge of Harlem at West 135th Street and Convent Avenue. It housed a two–story auditorium, a two–story gymnasium, and featured large window bays filled with unusual folding–casement steel sash windows, doorways with Tudor arches, and an exterior façade capped by parapets with crenellation and finials in the shape of creatures bearing shields. No wonder it became known as 'The Castle on the Hill'. But at the time it was also being used in part by another public school, and it served as an annex of the Wadleigh High School for girls.

Using a dozen vacant rooms in the building, The High School of Music and Art was formally dedicated on February 14, 1936. Mayor LaGuardia declared that, *"I believe that this is one of the best contributions which I will be able to make to the educational system of the city as long as I am Mayor of New York."* He would later declare it to be *"the most hopeful accomplishment"* of his administration.

The curriculum provided the basics of a 'regular' high school education — English, history, science, foreign languages, mathematics, and physical education — plus an additional three periods a day of music and art. During the first two years the art students were given a broad general introduction to all the arts, and the music students were given voice and instrumental training as well as courses in composition, musical theory, harmony, and choral singing. In the last two years they were allowed to focus more on their specific field of interest.

The second academic class of the high school started in September 1936, and in February 1937 Bobby Brittain became a freshman in the school's third class. Another member of his class was Bess Myerson who went on to become Miss America in 1945 and a popular television personality during the 1950s and 1960s.

For some students it was an unpleasant shock to suddenly be in a setting where everyone was as talented as they were. As one student wrote in the school paper:

Before we came to Music and Art, we tended to feel superior to those around us and to act as though we were too good for the world. Now that we have reached Music and Art, we find that the word 'genius' is abolished from our vocabulary. Our aim has changed from the purely selfish aim of becoming great artists to a sincere desire to share with others the beauty and happiness we find in music and art.

For Bobby it was an invigorating environment where his singing talent could be nurtured and where he was respected and appreciated enough to became president of his class. Outside of his classes in 'Voice Culture', he was especially drawn to his science courses and he soon became president of the school's Science Club. Although Bobby would be forced by family circumstances to drop out of this high school after only two years, he would continue to be captivated by the study of science and philosophy for the rest of his life.

Trivia:
– After winning a drawing at his high school Tommy got to visit Princeton University's *Institute for Advanced Studies* for a day. During this visit he heard Albert Einstein give a speech.
– Because of his interest in physics, Tommy was made an honorary member of the American Institute of Science while he was still a teenager.

MAJOR BOWES' ORIGINAL AMATEUR HOUR:

The former manager of WHN, the Loew's radio station that broadcast *The Bowery Mission Service* every week, was Edward 'Major' Bowes (he had been a Major in the Army Reserve during World War I). In 1934 Major Bowes had created a show called *The Amateur Hour* that, by 1937, was being broadcast by CBS to over 90 radio stations around the country. It was consistently ranked by industry surveys as one of the most popular shows on the air, and while most of the world was still in the grip of The Great Depression Major Bowes was making $2 million a year.

Around the time Bobby was accepted into The High School of Music and Art, he wrote a letter to Major Bowes applying for the show and comparing himself to a cross between Nelson Eddy and Lawrence Tibbett (a famous opera singer and recording artist). It was an enormous gamble because the show received over 10,000 applications a week. From this pool only about 500 were actually auditioned, and of these only 20 performers or acts were chosen for each show.

Bobby succeeded in being selected for an audition and he impressed everyone with his powerful,

Edward 'Major' Bowes
Host of *The Original Amateur Hour*

mature singing voice. He especially impressed Bessie Mack who was Major Bowes' secretary, press director, and overall 'right–hand man'. No one got on *The Amateur Hour* unless Bessie Mack said so, and when she heard Bobby Brittain she quickly gave him the 'thumbs up'. (In 1949 Tommy would appear, with many other former contestants who had become successful in Show Business, in a broadcast tribute to Bessie arranged by her son Ted Mack who had taken over *The Original Amateur Hour*.)

Before the show, contestants were given $10 and an all–you–can–eat meal card for the Bickford's cafeteria located across the street from the theater. They were also required to sign a contract stating that they would not use Bowes' name or their appearance on his show to secure future bookings. If they did happen to get work as a result of his show, they had to pay Bowes 15% of whatever money they earned.

The Amateur Hour was broadcast every Thursday night from the stage of the CBS Radio Theatre (1697 Broadway at West 53rd Street) in front of a large studio audience. To add an element of human interest to the show Major Bowes would interview each

NOW LISTEN TO A BROADCAST
AS THE *Control* MAN HEARS IT!

**HEAR YOUR FAVORITE
RADIO PROGRAM AS PERFECTLY
AS THE ENGINEER IN
THE CONTROL ROOM**

HERE'S where the *experts* go to listen! Not in the studio, but in the private control room, where reception is perfect. Here, each subtle tone is perfectly reproduced, just as it goes on the air. That's radio at its best—just as you now can hear it in your home with the new 1936 Atwater Kent, the Radio with Control-Room Reception!

MAJOR BOWES and one of his young guests on his amateur hour, radio's most outstanding program.

How new Arrow-Light Tuning and special tone controls
bring in programs clearer than ever before

FIVE-TUBE CONSOLE with metal tubes. (Shown above in illustration.) New Arrow-Light Tuning. New Rainbow Dial. Improved standard and short-wave reception. Ask to see Model 335.

NEW ARROW-LIGHT TUNING... NEW RAINBOW DIAL
Makes those hard-to-get stations easier to tune in. Makes local stations clearer, better. Accurate as a stop watch. Old-fashioned "glare" dial now replaced by beautiful, illuminated Rainbow Dial.

SIX-METAL-TUBE COMPACT. (At right) An amazing small set for foreign and domestic programs. New Arrow-Light Tuning. New Rainbow Dial. Ask to see Model 456.

Prices range from $24.50 to $160.00 f.o.b. factory and are subject to change without notice.

YOU can't hear a program *right* if you can't tune in properly. On the new Atwater Kent, the flashing colors of its new Rainbow Dial, and the new moving Arrow-Light, lead you straight to the heart of your favorite program. No more blurred tuning. Full, rich, perfect program tone.

What's more, you get special tone controls, automatic volume control, and on larger sets a Selectivity-Fidelity switch

—really a Control Room in miniature—when you own the new Atwater Kent, the ideal radio for standard and short-wave reception.

Do this: Go to your Atwater Kent dealer. Ask for an Atwater Kent in your home, where you can hear and enjoy it. Listen to foreign programs. Listen to local stations. By any test, you'll pick the new Atwater Kent, the Radio with Control-Room Reception.

ATWATER KENT MANUFACTURING COMPANY   A. Atwater Kent, *President*   Philadelphia, Pa.

ATWATER KENT
THE RADIO WITH *Control-Room Reception*

contestant for a few minutes before they performed. These supposedly spontaneous interviews were actually scripted and rehearsed. When the interview was over the actual performance would begin. If a performer didn't do well or his act wasn't very good, Major Bowes would strike a bell (the kind used at boxing matches) while saying "all right, all right" and the performer would be immediately whisked away from the microphone and off the stage, usually to the delight of the audience.

Trivia:
– Edward 'Major' Bowes was born on June 14, 1874. He was 60 years old when he created *The Amateur Hour*. (So many other radio shows began imitating the format of his show, that he soon changed the name to *The Original Amateur Hour*.) Major Bowes died June 13, 1946.
– Major Bowes lived above the Loew's Capitol Theatre in a 14–room apartment filled with expensive art and antiques. He also owned a palatial country home overlooking the Hudson River.
– In 1936 *The Amateur Hour* was the first show to be broadcast from the CBS Radio Theatre (also called the 'Columbia Radio Theatre' and the 'CBS Radio Playhouse No. 1'). It had been originally built in 1927 as Hammerstein's Theatre, and is now called The Ed Sullivan Theater.

Through phone calls and postcards the New York City radio audience (and the audience from an "honor city" that had been chosen for that week) would vote for their favorite performance and determine which artist or act was that week's winner. A phone bank staffed by over 50 operators handled the incoming calls during the show, registering the votes and sending them to tabulators. Winners were announced the following week and sometimes asked back. (According to AT&T the show received 2,562,837 phone calls during its first two years on the air.)

Bobby's speaking voice was very childlike, and during his on–air interview he told Major Bowes where he went to school and a little about his life. He also told Major Bowes that he was twelve–years–old, even though he was already thirteen, because his mother thought it would make his singing even more impressive. Then Bobby read a poem he had written — a rather dark poem about being in the grave — before singing the song they had picked for him. The song, titled "That's Why Darkies Are Born", was from the 1931 musical revue "George White's Scandals" and originally sung by the popular opera baritone Everett Marshall. Today, of course, the song would be considered politically incorrect and never allowed on the radio, but it must be remembered that at the time such shows as *Amos 'n' Andy* were extremely popular and this song was considered part of the standard repertory for singers, both black and white.

The contrast between Bobby's childlike speaking voice and his deep, powerful rendition of the song astonished both the theater and radio audiences. All the phones began ringing and the operators were inundated with a flood of votes for this young baritone. The number of votes for Bobby was so impressive that the show's producer came over to where he was sitting and asked if he would sing another song. Bobby was told they were going to cancel the final act so he could sing an encore. So it was that this thirteen–year–old boy with the amazing voice sang "Chloe" as an encore for a national audience and returned the following week to sing again.

Tommy's First Publicity Photo (c. 1938)

THE CREATION OF 'TOMMY DIX':

Now that Bobby was receiving proper training at The High School of Music and Art, and with his success on *The Original Amateur Hour* appearing to be the first step on his road to stardom, Bobby's mother and her sisters were absolutely convinced that he would become rich and famous if he received the proper help and support.

Bobby's aunts Dolly (Doris Meyer) and Sally (Sally Olkin) owned a shop at 362 5th Avenue called the Navard Specialty Company. (It was located in Midtown Manhattan right around the corner from the Empire State Building.) One year they came up with an idea that proved to be very profitable. At the beginning of each Christmas season they would visit the CEOs of large companies in the area and offer to choose, wrap, and address the gifts that the CEOs wanted to give. This took the burden off the CEOs, and once Dolly and Sally demonstrated how easy the process was they were almost always hired again in the following years. Bobby's aunts met a lot of important people this way, and they used their contacts to learn about opportunities for their nephew and to get advice.

One of the opportunities they directed Bobby toward was the monthly meeting of The Studio Salon. Founded by Cordelia Ayer Paine, this organization for society women met in the Historic Arts Galleries at the Astor Hotel to discuss cultural topics, review literary trends, listen to lectures and readings, and hear some refined entertainment. On September 11, 1938, Cordelia Paine invited two baritones to sing for the group — Wallace Mattice and Bobby Brittain. Bobby's family felt such appearances were a very good way to become known among important people.

Another opportunity that Bobby took advantage of was the auditions held by Madge Tucker at NBC. Madge managed all of the children's programs for NBC Radio, acting in various capacities as either producer, director, writer, host, or even on occasion, music arranger. Twice a month she would hold open auditions for any child under the age of 17, and usually between 50 and 60 children would show up for the tryouts. Of these, however, only three or four would demonstrate enough talent to be hired for one of her programs. Once hired, Madge would use her programs as a training camp for the aspiring young entertainers, teaching them how to read lines from a script and how to perform in front of a microphone. Many of these children went on to notable careers in Show Business after they graduated from Madge's 'Radio School'.

Bobby and his mother decided that he should go to one of Madge's auditions, but first Bobby's mother was persuaded to choose a better stage name for him. Exactly why and when this happened has been lost in the mist of Time. It is known that for a long time Bobby's extended family felt that the name Bobby Brittain was too easily confused with Bobby Breen, a popular young soprano who was the leading

Madge Tucker (1935)
NBC Radio's Director of Children's Programs

juvenile star at RKO Radio Pictures at the time. Two boy singers with similar sounding names didn't seem like a good idea. A number of new names were offered to Bobby's mother by her sisters and others, and it's possible that Dolly and Sally received some valuable advice about this question from one of the CEOs they were dealing with who had Show Business connections. Whatever the circumstances, Bobby's mother narrowed the list of names down to three and asked Bobby to choose one. When Bobby saw the name 'Tommy Dix' he knew immediately that would be his new name. Audiences, from that point on, would know the former Bobby Brittain only as Tommy Dix.

Auditioning for Madge Tucker sometime in early 1939, Tommy Dix was quickly hired to appear on both *Coast to Coast on a Bus* and *Our Barn*. *Coast to Coast on a Bus* used over a dozen children each week to entertain the young listening audience with music, singing, stories, and poetry — all while supposedly riding The White Rabbit Bus. Milton Cross, who served as the show's host (the 'conductor' of the bus), was also the host of the Metropolitan Opera's radio broadcasts every Saturday afternoon. *Our Barn* was a storytelling program directed by Madge Tucker where children played the characters in the story, acting out the parts.

Tommy soon became part of each show's regular company and, perhaps more importantly, he was *paid* for his appearances. His first check, signed by the advertising agency Young and Rubicam, officially made him a 'professional'. (He was paid $20.00 for performing on the radio, but a small amount was withheld because of the new Social Security tax.)

Unfortunately, it wasn't long after this that Tommy's mother fell ill and she wasn't able to support them as she had done in the past. Although it was a hard, painful decision, Tommy decided to leave The High School of Music and Art after only two years and "commercialize on whatever talent I had." He began to play young people on other radio shows like *Renfrew of the Mounted*, *The Aldrich Family*, *Superman*, and the daytime soap opera *The Life and Love of Doctor Susan*. (On *Doctor Susan* he played the tough kid Bumstead Brice. Tommy had to get permission from his mother to see one of *The Dead End Kids* movies so he'd know how to sound tough.)

But Tommy's true passion was singing, and he looked for any opportunity to showcase his amazing voice. One day an unusual opportunity to sing in front of a prestigious audience unexpectedly came his way when he decided he would do something for President Roosevelt's crusade to find a cure for the disease of Infantile Paralysis.

THE 'MARCH OF DIMES':
Tommy and his mother were great admirers of the President of the United States, Franklin Delano Roosevelt. Each January 30th, on the President's birthday, Birthday Balls

were held across the country to raise money for the fight against the disease of Infantile Paralysis (commonly referred to as polio). In 1937 The National Foundation for Infantile Paralysis was created, and the radio appeal that occurred during the week preceding the Birthday Ball events was named 'The March of Dimes'.

Sometime during 1938 Tommy told his mother that he wanted to do something special for FDR and the newly named 'March of Dimes' campaign, and his mother suggested that he write a song. Although he had never written a song before, Tommy began to compose the words (he had already written a number of poems) and eventually he plucked out a tune for his lyrics on an old piano. The following year, with song in hand, Tommy went to the Brill Building just north of Times Square where scores of music publishers had offices. With the guilelessness of youth Tommy went from one office to the next until he found a music publisher who agreed to publish the song, but only if Tommy could get invited to sing it during the next President's Ball at the Waldorf–Astoria Hotel.

Wasting no time, Tommy proceeded to the headquarters of George V. Riley, the chairman of the Greater New York Committee in charge of organizing the 1940 President's Ball in Manhattan. Without an appointment, but with youthful pluck and confidence, Tommy went up to the receptionist and burst into song. His stentorian delivery immediately caught the attention of everyone in the Committee's suite of offices, including Mr. Riley. Mr. Riley invited Tommy into his office and he quickly recognized the appeal that this diminutive young boy with the amazing voice would have. Without further ado he invited Tommy to perform his "March of Dimes" song at the next President's Ball.

On January 30, 1940, 16–year–old Tommy Dix attended the President's Ball at the Waldorf–Astoria Hotel dressed in his Boy

George V. Riley (1940)
'President's Ball' Chairman for Greater NY

Scout uniform. The President's mother, Sara Roosevelt, and two thousand guests watched as a legion of Boy Scouts and Girl Scouts marched into the ballroom led by a drum and bugle corps. Then, according to *The New York Times*, after a ballet by The Chalif Dancers and an aria by Ladis Kiepura, a Polish operatic tenor, *"The climax was effectively reached*

The March of Dimes

Words and Music by
TOMMY DIX

when Tommy Dix, 14–year–old [sic] *Boy Scout baritone, sang his own composition, 'The March of Dimes', a copy of which he presented to the President's mother."*

Tommy then led the entire audience in a rendition of "Happy Birthday" while the enormous birthday cake was being cut. After the show Sara Roosevelt came backstage and spoke with Tommy for a few minutes indicating he would be invited to the White House the following year to sing his song. For a number of reasons his appearance at the White House never took place, but Tommy would sing his "March of Dimes" song again during the 1942 President's Birthday Ball at the Waldorf–Astoria where the newly published sheet music for his song was sold to raise money for the campaign.

THE METROPOLITAN OPERA AUDITIONS OF THE AIR (1940):

After his appearance at the Waldorf–Astoria Hotel Tommy was invited to sing his "March of Dimes" song on a number of occasions during the following months. His song made such a lasting impression that even three years later, after the movie he co–starred in was released, Tommy was still often described in the newspapers as *"the lad who wrote the March of Dimes song for President Roosevelt's birthday party."*

The following October Tommy was walking past NBC's studio 8–H when he heard a group of singers getting ready to try out for a radio program called *The Metropolitan Opera Auditions of the Air*. Every year, from October through March, aspiring operatic performers would compete to sing on the show in front of a panel of judges for a $1,000 prize and a contract to perform with the Metropolitan Opera. Tommy asked if he could 'horn in' on the tryouts, and when he sang "Old Man River" for the show's judges they were both startled and impressed. After the audition was over they decided to put Tommy on the show as a special guest because he was too young to compete. In its November 11th issue, *TIME* magazine reported the incident in a short article that began:

> **In an NBC studio in Manhattan, a squad of baritones warmed up. Said a sharp–eared passer–by to a receptionist: "Is there a job open for baritones? Maybe I can horn in on this audition." Horn in he did. When he sang before Conductor Wilfrid Pelletier and other judges of the Metropolitan Opera Auditions of the Air — a Sunday program from which two singers annually are chosen for small places in the opera — he impressed them vastly. Last Sunday they put him on the auditions program — but as a guest, not a contestant. Even if Baritone Tommy Dix won a job, the Metropolitan would be hard put to find him work. He is only 15 years old** [sic]**. But on the radio the Met's Manager Edward Johnson introduced him as a singer of promise and let him carol Malotte's lusty "Song of the Open Road".**

If 1940 was a pivotal year in Tommy Dix's unfolding singing career, October and November were the pivotal months. During those two months he was not only chosen to sing on the third show of the prestigious *Metropolitan Opera Auditions of the Air*, but the 'door of opportunity' swung wide open when a chance encounter with Ezra Stone put him on the path to Broadway. Ezra Stone was the star of the popular radio comedy *The Aldrich Family*. He had always liked Tommy and was instrumental in getting Tommy parts on both his and other radio programs.

This chance encounter, as it happened, also took place in October when Tommy was using a piano in one of NBC's empty studios to rehearse some of his favorite songs. Ezra happened to walk in and was dazzled by Tommy's singing.

"I didn't know you could sing," he said.

"Actually, it's what I enjoy doing the most," Tommy replied.

"You're very good. You might want to try out for a part in a play they're currently casting on Broadway. I'm told they need some young singers." Ezra gave Tommy the name of the show's producer and his address. Tommy didn't waste any time making an appointment with the man Ezra recommended, a Mr. Herman Shumlin.

Herman Shumlin had obtained the American rights to *The Corn is Green*, a heartwarming British drama that had previously run in London for two years. The storyline takes place in a small Welsh village in the late 1800s and Ethel Barrymore had agreed to play the show's central character, a schoolteacher named Miss Moffat. A number of teenagers were going to be needed for the cast, and the teenagers would have to sing some Welsh songs during the play.

Shumlin, the show's producer/director, hired Tommy after his interview and audition even though Tommy confessed he didn't know how to speak with a Welsh accent, and didn't even know what a Welsh accent sounded like. Tommy was elated! He was not only going to be appearing in a Broadway play at the tender age of sixteen, he was going to be on the same stage as the legendary Ethel Barrymore.

24

BOYS IN THE NEWS

1. MODEL NAVY: This 18½" model of the aircraft carrier Lexington is the largest unit of a 51 ship fleet, exhibited by the Navy, and whittled by William M. Tompkins, 17 yr. old Hollywood, Calif., student.

2. NEW MAYOR: Sam Breci, a member of the Boys' Town band and football team, was recently elected Mayor of Boys' Town, from which office he directs the Boys' Town government and greets all newcomers.

3. TO ENTER COLLEGE: Alexander Hull Jr., 12 yr. old scholar, will enter the University of Washington next quarter as the youngest student enrolled in the student body of the University.

4. WINS ORATORICAL PRIZE: Frank Church Jr., 16 yr. old high school student of Boise, Idaho, won the $4000 scholarship in the American Legion's National Americanism Oratorical Contest.

5. YOUNG RADIO STAR: Tommy Dix, 16 yr. old baritone, radio and stage actor, appeared on NBC's Metropolitan Auditions of the air, the youngest contestant ever to sing on the program by eight years.

6. GIFT FOR PRESIDENT: Teddy Kulikowski, age 8 yrs., brought some of his wood carvings to the White House, and is all smiles as he turns the carvings over to Brig. Gen. Edwin Watson, White House Aide.

7. NEW SCIENTIST: Wallace Cloud, 14 yr. old student member of the American Institute's new laboratory, is studying the distilling of garbage with the expectation that it will yield valuable chemicals.

In the June 1941 issue of *Boys' Life* magazine, Tommy Dix (#5) is one of the "Boys in the News"

Chapter 3

BROADWAY

THE CORN IS GREEN (1940):

By the end of 1940 the world was in a state of turmoil. Hitler had invaded Poland, Norway, Denmark, the Netherlands, Belgium, Luxembourg, and France, and London was being bombed daily by Germany's Luftwaffe. Although the United States was still officially neutral, isolationists were losing ground and it was becoming clear that America would eventually have to join the growing conflict. Germany, Italy, and Japan signed a treaty in September that made the three countries allies against England and France. In October Italy invaded Greece, and German troops came to the Italians' aid.

New York City's Theater District was experiencing troubles of its own. The crippling economic effects of The Great Depression; the exodus of theatrical talent (actors, directors, and writers) from New York City to Hollywood; the lure of live vaudeville shows that accompanied screenings of new movies in the ornate downtown picture palaces; the growing attraction of nightclub shows that featured famous entertainers; and the lack of originality in many new stage productions, all contributed to dwindling ticket sales for legitimate shows and an increase in the number of plays that quickly failed. This also held true for musicals and revues. As Ethan Mordden observes in his book *Beautiful Mornin'*, "*The Broadway musical had been running on empty for years.*"

Indeed, this deteriorating situation had spanned the entire decade of the 1930s, and 1940 was the eleventh successive year the number of new plays had declined on Broadway. During the 1930/1931 theatrical season, for instance, 187 shows opened on 'The Great White Way'. During the 1940/1941 season there were only 69 productions, and most of them didn't make any money. Many new plays failed within three weeks, and a drama called *Gabrielle* (an adaptation of Thomas Mann's short story *Tristan*) opened at the end of the season on March 25th, 1941, and closed the next day.

One of the bright spots of the 1940/1941 Broadway season, however, was the premiere of the semi–autobiographical British play *The Corn is Green*. Originally produced in London in 1938, this 'intelligent comedy' (LIFE magazine's description) was forced to close in England after a successful two years because of the German air raids. Now on Broadway, with Ethel Barrymore taking over the lead role as a spinster schoolteacher, the show received rave reviews and was almost immediately playing to standing–room–only audiences. Typical of the reviews was this one written by Mark Barron that said, in part:

Miss Barrymore has fulfilled abundantly the hopes of her followers. She has returned to town in a brilliant, heart–warming play from England called The Corn Is Green. Her performance was cheered by critics and playgoers with an enthusiasm usually reserved for brilliant newcomers.

The scene of the play is a mining community in Wales. To this settlement comes a compassionate schoolma'am (Miss Barrymore). She is determined to improve the condition of the children of the impoverished, unlettered miners. One of the lads is discovered to have extraordinary literary talents, and upon him the teacher centers her instructions.

This sums up to a story of the utmost simplicity. The reward of the lad is a scholarship to Oxford, as it was in the real life case of author Williams, and the scholarship is received by the student because the teacher is determined above everything else that this talented student will get the education to improve the lives of the little people among whom he lives.

This is, incidentally, the first play of the current season to win the unqualified acclaim of both the first–nighters and critics.

The Broadway cast of *The Corn is Green* (1940)

The play opened at the National Theatre on November 26, 1940. Tommy was cast as one of the teenagers attending the school set up by Ethel Barrymore's character for the disadvantaged children working in the local coal mine. He had one or two lines in the play (spoken in Welsh) and with the other 'students' he sang Welsh songs *a cappella* from both on and off the stage. Songs such as "Bugeilio'r Gwenyth Gwyn" and "Yr Hugen Melyn" were not only mastered by Tommy, they made such an impression on him that he is still able to sing them. In addition to playing one of Miss Moffat's students, Tommy also understudied one of the larger speaking parts. He was paid $50 a week.

Sidney Shalett of the *New York Times* interviewed Ethel Barrymore a month after *The Corn is Green* opened on Broadway. After the interview he wrote the following:

> **But the important current news from Miss Barrymore was her declaration, made freely and without qualification, that she considered her current role as Miss Moffat in Emlyn Williams's "The Corn is Green" by far the greatest part she ever has had. Indeed, she inferred, it may be her last role, for she is convinced that the play is so fine that it well may go on forever, between Broadway and the road. Leaning forward a bit, and looking more and more like her equally famous brother Lionel, Miss Barrymore emphatically asserted:**
>
> **"I like it better than anything I've ever had. It has everything in it that I care about."**

That year *The Corn is Green* won The New York Drama Critics Award for "Best Foreign Play", and LIFE magazine published four pages of photographs from the play in an article that enthused, *"As teacher Moffat, Ethel Barrymore at 61 gives the least mannered, most heart–warming performance of her career, supported by an expert cast directed by Herman Shumlin."*

The play stayed on Broadway until January 17, 1942, (477 performances) and then toured around the country for over two years.

Trivia:
– Broadway ticket prices for *The Corn is Green* ranged from $1.10 to $3.30.
– When Tommy left the show at the end of the summer of 1941, his part was eventually filled by the young actor Tony Randall.
– In 1945 *The Corn is Green* was made into a film starring Bette Davis.
– In 1979 a made–for–television movie of *The Corn is Green*, starring Katharine Hepburn, was filmed on location in Wales.

BEST FOOT FORWARD (1941):

At the end of 1941 the world and Broadway were both much as they had been at the end of the previous year. The drums of war were still sounding around the world; America was still neutral, although that would suddenly change on December 7th when Japan attacked the U.S. naval base at Pearl Harbor and three days later Germany and Italy declared war on the United States; and although 83 productions opened on Broadway, only 12 of them made a profit by the end of the season.

Sometime during the summer of 1941, while *The Corn Is Green* was still playing on Broadway, Tommy learned from his friend Ezra Stone that George Abbott, who had just produced the successful musical *Pal Joey*, was auditioning young singers and dancers for a new musical comedy called *Best Foot Forward*. Written by John Cecil Holm, and co–produced by Richard Rodgers, the play was set in a Pennsylvania boys' prep school and would feature a cast of young, unknown performers.

Tommy auditioned for Abbott and his staff and received the standard request to leave his phone number so they could call him if he was needed. Tommy was unaware that his powerful voice had caught the attention of Abbott and the two 27–year–old composers who had written the score for the show, Hugh Martin and Ralph Blane. Along with thirteen other songs, Martin and Blane had written a school fight song that they felt would be perfect for Tommy.

The Broadway cast of *Best Foot Forward* (1941)

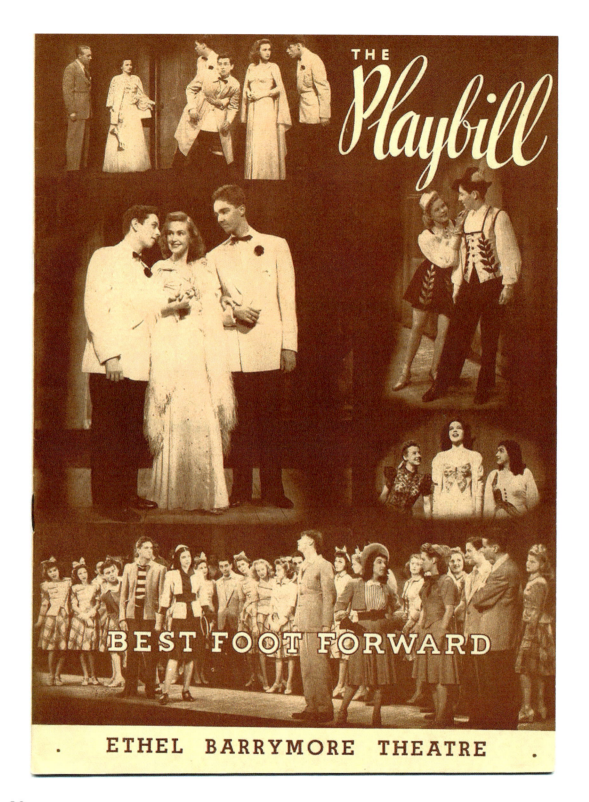

THE Playbill

BEST FOOT FORWARD

ETHEL BARRYMORE THEATRE

According to the book *Beautiful Mornin'* by Ethan Mordden:

> **Best Foot Forward** is no more than who's dating whom, who's
> breaking up, and who's probably going to reconcile. But then, that's this
> show's peculiar charm: a long, loving look at what matters to carefree
> kids.
>
> Historian Stanley Green informs us that it was Rodgers who gave
> *Best Foot Forward*'s prep school its famous name, for the show had gone
> into rehearsal without anyone's being able to come up with a suitable
> sound for this place of youth in merry riot. The school's fight song had
> been written around a working title "Wisconsin". This became "Tioga",
> but that felt like . . . well, the musical comedy version of a prep school.
> "What we need," said Abbott, "is a name that has something to do with
> winning with a lot of sock in it." "That's it!" said Rodgers, " 'Winsocki.' "

So the fight song that had been tentatively titled "Buckle Down, Tioga" now
became "Buckle Down, Winsocki". Tommy was called back and told he would be cast as
Chuck Green, a small part but one that would feature him singing the school's fight song
at the opening of the second act, and he would understudy the part of the lead character.

Many years later Tommy learned that on opening night, after the first act was
over, George Abbott felt the show was a flop. The audience response had been lackluster,
and the show didn't seem to have any punch. Then the curtain rose for the second act,
and Tommy's powerful baritone voice rang out with the rousing fight song "Buckle Down,
Winsocki." When he came to the end of the song and began to walk off stage the
audience rose to its feet with a thunderous standing ovation, and the stage manager
turned to Tommy and said, "Go out and take a bow, son, you're a star now!"

Tommy's rendition of that song proved to be the spark that ignited the play, a
point that was emphasized by Hugh Martin in a letter to Tommy dated October 4, 2001,
which reads in part:

> George Abbott has told me several times that the show might
> have failed if it hadn't been for you. He said that until you stepped
> forward to sing "Winsocki" he was not at all sure which way the wind was
> going to blow. After you stopped the show for us, he told me he knew
> we were going to be a smash!

Hugh Martin officially acknowledged the importance of Tommy's rendition of
"Buckle Down, Winsocki" in his 2010 memoir *Hugh Martin: The Boy Next Door*:

Page 147:

Mr. Abbott told me later that at intermission opening night he wasn't sure as to the fate of the show, whether it would hit or miss. "It was 'Winsocki' that made the difference," he said. "The curtain went up on the second act, and two minutes later little Tommy Dix was belting out 'Winsocki' and suddenly I knew we were in."

Pages 149–150:

[On opening night] I mustered enough courage to go backstage at intermission . . . Were we clicking? Did they like it? Would we be a hit?

The Entr'acte started up and each of us scurried to wherever we belonged. Me, of course, sitting on the steps, trying to convince myself that I was breathing.

The curtain rose on Act Two, and after about six or eight innocuous lines of dialogue, pint–sized Tommy Dix began to sing "Buckle Down, Winsocki" backed up by the entire cast, plus a rousing orchestration. It was a great moment for all of us because "Winsocki" neatly wrapped up the show and put it in the smash category. For Ralph, it must have been an impossible dream come true, because "Winsocki" is and always was his personal brainchild. We were all winners together, but the special heroes that night were Tommy Dix, singing Ralph's marvelous and very original song, Gene Kelly's ingenious and lively dances, and the adorable Nancy Walker.

Although the initial reviews were mixed, the musical proved to be a success. But even those reviewers who felt, *"Twenty minutes or half an hour of Best Foot Forward was enough,"* singled out Nancy Walker and Tommy Dix for special praise. Soon after the play opened a reviewer for the *New Yorker* magazine wrote, *"If 'Buckle Down, Winsocki' isn't the best school song in America, I wish you'd name one."*

A few days after the premiere of *Best Foot Forward*, George Abbott arranged to have Tommy record "Buckle Down, Winsocki" with Benny Goodman and His Orchestra. On the flip side of the record Peggy Lee sang another song from the musical, "Shady Lady Bird" (a song that was not used in the movie). The 78rpm record was an immediate hit around the country. "Buckle Down, Winsocki" became one of the more popular songs of the early 1940s and, from that moment on, was forever identified with Tommy Dix.

Toward the end of *Best Foot Forward*'s run, Arthur Freed came to New York City and attended a matinee performance of the show. Arthur Freed was the head of the Metro–Goldwyn–Mayer unit in charge of producing the movie studio's musicals, and he

Tommy Dix (1941)   *PHOTOFEST*

liked *Best Foot Forward*. Although Harry Cohn, the head of Columbia Pictures, had initially offered to purchase the play's movie rights, Arthur Freed out–bid him and M–G–M bought the rights to the musical for $150,000. In addition to hiring the young composers Hugh Martin and Ralph Blane, Arthur Freed decided to bring some of the young Broadway cast to Hollywood to do the movie version. That group included Gil Stratton (the male lead), June Allyson, Nancy Walker, Jack Jordan, Kenny Bowers, and Tommy Dix.

Trivia:

– *Best Foot Forward* opened on Broadway October 1, 1941, and ran for 326 performances.

– The top ticket price for *Best Foot Forward* was $6.60.

– The editors of LIFE magazine ran a five–page article about *Best Foot Forward* in their October 13, 1941, issue that included nine photographs of the show.

– Tommy was initially paid $50 per week to be in *Best Foot Forward*. Once his rendition of "Buckle Down, Winsocki" became a hit, his salary was increased to $65 per week.

– The tune from the song "Buckle Down, Winsocki" was used for the 1970's *Buckle Up For Safety* public service announcements.

– Gene Kelly did the choreography for the show and also served as the show's Assistant Director. He left for Hollywood the day after *Best Foot Forward* opened on Broadway.

– In her autobiography June Allyson says that George Abbott chose her to be in *Best Foot Forward* because he needed "a funny girl to ham up some scenes with Nancy Walker."

– Hugh Martin and Ralph Blane each earned between $400 — $500 per week while *Best Foot Forward* was on Broadway.

– Ralph Blane's real last name was Hunsecker.

– Hugh Martin graduated from the Birmingham Conservatory of Music in Birmingham, Alabama.

– Harry Cohn had wanted to buy the movie rights to *Best Foot Forward* for Rita Hayworth and Shirley Temple.

– Two months after *Best Foot Forward* opened on Broadway the Japanese attacked Pearl Harbor and the U.S. entered World War II.

– There was a revival of *Best Foot Forward* on April 2, 1963, at Stage 73 in New York City. Included in the cast were Liza Minnelli and Christopher Walken (who was billed as Ronald Walken).

Once *Best Foot Forward* had settled into its Broadway run, Tommy's bestselling record and show–stopping performance began bringing numerous inquiries and offers to appear and sing. One of the offers he accepted was a booking at the famous Copacabana nightclub just down the street from the Ethel Barrymore Theatre where *Best Foot Forward* was playing. Each night after his Broadway show was over, Tommy would walk over to the Copacabana and sing in their late show. He was such a hit that when *Best Foot Forward* closed on Broadway in July 1942, Tommy was hired to sing at the Ritz Carlton in Boston for six weeks. He then went to Chicago where he appeared with the touring company of *Best Foot Forward* before finally heading for Hollywood.

Trivia:

– Up until the 1960s, Boston's Ritz–Carlton Hotel was regarded as a private
  club for the very wealthy. Guests were regularly checked to see if they
  were in the Social Register or *Who's Who*, and the hotel sometimes
  went so far as to examine the quality of writing paper on which the
  guests wrote to the hotel requesting reservations. (If the paper wasn't
  of high enough quality, they were refused a reservation.)

– Tommy used his sudden celebrity status to help schools and
  organizations raise money for various charities. He has continued these
  charitable performances throughout his life.

Chapter 4

HOLLYWOOD

Tommy Dix and other cast members from *Best Foot Forward* were probably unaware of the war's effects on Hollywood as they boarded trains to Los Angeles in the winter of 1942, but the effects were widespread and profound.

The Office of War Information (OWI) was formed in June 1942, and given unprecedented control over the content of American motion pictures so they would properly depict America's social and political issues, its allies and enemies, and its role in the envisioned postwar world. The export of films that showed racial discrimination, depicted Americans as single–handedly winning the war, or painted our allies as imperialists, was prohibited.

The OWI's office for domestic operations, the Bureau of Motion Pictures (BMP), imposed allotments on raw film stock that was about 25% below the studios' 1941 usage. Restrictions were also imposed on everything from expenditures for new sets (limited to $5,000 per picture), to how much material could be used for costumes, to what could be spent on transportation. The studios even had to find a substitute for the rubber used to create fake cobwebs on their sets because of the shortage of rubber.

By October of 1942, around 2,700 Hollywood people — 12% of the total number employed in the movie industry — had joined the armed forces. The following month the draft age was lowered from 21 to 18, requiring even Tommy to sign up with his local draft board in New York City. Many of those left behind in Hollywood spent time touring the country selling war bonds and entertaining the troops, and that fall The Hollywood Canteen was opened in Los Angeles as a morale booster. Staffed by a rotating list of Hollywood's most famous performers, The Hollywood Canteen provided free entertainment, food, and comradeship to servicemen going overseas.

However, despite all of these disruptions, shortages, and restrictions, the war was good for Hollywood's profits. Before the war, in 1941, the combined profits of Hollywood's eight largest studios were $35 million. In 1942 that figure rose to nearly $50 million, and held at almost $60 million for the next three years.

Those generous profits, however, didn't filter down very much to Hollywood's new recruits from New York City. June Allyson recalls in her autobiography that when she arrived at Metro–Goldwyn–Mayer (M–G–M) she was paid $125 per week, less 10% to her agent. But she was only paid if she was actually working in a movie. Fortunately, almost as soon as she arrived she was given a part in the Mickey Rooney movie *Girl Crazy* that began filming before *Best Foot Forward* was ready to shoot, so she didn't have to wait long to be put on M–G–M's payroll.

THE WILLIAM MORRIS AGENCY:

By the late 1930s the William Morris Agency was one of the largest and most important talent and literary agencies in the country with offices in New York City, London, Chicago, and Los Angeles. They had several hundred actors and entertainers on their roster who produced earnings for the agency of over $15 million a year. Motion pictures accounted for a third of their revenue; radio brought in another third; and the rest came from nine other departments — vaudeville, literary, nightclubs, Broadway shows, bands, etc.

When they arrived in Hollywood, Tommy Dix, his close friend Nancy Walker, and one or two others decided that they needed an agent. All of them had heard of the William Morris Agency, and they decided to visit the Agency's Los Angeles offices and sign up. The William Morris Agency was always searching for fresh, new talent, and these cast members from the Broadway musical were just what they were looking for. It didn't take long for Tommy and the rest to sign contracts, and the William Morris Agency would represent Tommy until the late 1940s.

TOMMY IS GIVEN THE LEAD ROLE:

As soon as M–G–M obtained the movie rights to the Broadway musical *Best Foot Forward*, Arthur Freed's unit and the studio's writers started working on the screenplay. While the screenplay followed the Broadway play's general plot fairly closely, some of the musical's songs were dropped and new ones were written. The location of the story was changed from a civilian prep school to a military academy (to give the movie a more patriotic flavor), and it was decided that the play's hit song "Buckle Down, Winsocki" should be moved to the end of the movie where it could provide a rousing finale. The production team also felt that it would

Arthur Freed

be better if the story's male lead sang the final song.

By the time Tommy Dix and his mother arrived in Hollywood, Arthur Freed was convinced that Tommy was the only person who could do justice to "Buckle Down, Winsocki". Besides, he had something else in mind for Gil Stratton, the male lead of the Broadway show.

Mickey Rooney and Judy Garland were preparing to make *Girl Crazy*, their last movie together. The actor Ray McDonald had been scheduled to play Mickey's roommate in the movie, but Ray had gone into the Army and was unavailable. Because of the war Hollywood was short of leading men, so in November 1942 Arthur Freed decided to have Gil Stratton play Mickey's roommate in *Girl Crazy* and move Tommy Dix into the leading role in *Best Foot Forward*. Both movies were to be shot at about the same time on M–G–M's backlots, but only *Best Foot Forward* would be shot in Technicolor.

In the book *Judy: A Legendary Film Career* by John Fricke, Gil Stratton is quoted as saying:

> **I came out from New York to do my role in *Best Foot Forward* for MGM — only to be told that Tommy Dix was going to play the part. Very dejected. I was called into Arthur Freed's office, and he told me, "*I'm going to put you into the next Judy–Mickey [picture] in place of Ray McDonald,*" who'd gone off to the war. Well, he was a dancer; I was a singer. But they said that was okay . . . and [then] I watched the music being doled out. I ended up with four bars of "Embraceable You"! And when I went to the sneak preview, all my funny lines were gone, too. In place after place, there was a dissolve or a cut or a fade–out, so I'm not in the picture very much, despite the billing. I ran into Al Akst, the editor, at the Brown Derby, and he explained, "*In a picture with Mickey Rooney, no other guy is going to get the laughs!*"**

WORKING AT THE METRO–GOLDWYN–MAYER STUDIOS:

It may have come as a surprise to Tommy and the rest of *Best Foot Forward's* New York cast that the Metro–Goldwyn–Mayer movie studio was not located in Hollywood. Despite the designation "Made in Hollywood, USA" that appeared on all of M–G–M's films, the vast studio complex was actually situated on 185 fenced and gated acres in Culver City, California, ten miles from Hollywood. This 'movie factory', built on six separate lots, was a self–contained "city within a city" and it is estimated that a fifth of all movies made in America before 1970 were shot on its sound stages and backlots.

Just navigating around the extensive property could be daunting, and if you entered the wrong gate by mistake you might quickly become lost. Administration buildings, a labyrinth of sound stages and offices, warehouses, standing sets of all descriptions, workshops, film labs, a huge power plant, and even a fire department and barbershop were just a few of the facilities crowded onto the grounds of the studio.

The film version of *Best Foot Forward* was shot at the M–G–M studio from January 18 to March 24, 1943. The actress playing the movie star who accepts a cadet's invitation to be his date at his school prom was originally going to be Lana Turner, but when she became pregnant Lucille Ball was given the part. The popular bandleader and trumpet virtuoso, Harry James, was hired to be in the movie, and during the climatic scene at the school prom he and his band performed memorable renditions of "Two O'clock Jump" (a variation on "One O'clock Jump") and "Flight of the Bumble Bee".

A number of scenes that took place indoors in the play were filmed outdoors for the movie, and those exterior scenes were shot at M–G–M's Lot Two using a standing set called 'Girl's School'. This backlot set was used whenever an academic campus was needed, and in slightly altered form it appeared in such diverse movies as *Love Laughs at Andy Hardy* (1946), *Good News* (1947), *Cynthia* (1947), *The Cobweb* (1955), *The Wings of Eagles* (1957), and *Mame* (1974) among many others.

M–G–M's 'Girl's School', a standing set located on Lot Two (shown in the mid–1960s)
This set was altered in various ways for each new movie. Here a clock tower has been added.

Trivia:

– Tommy was paid $400 per week to appear in *Best Foot Forward*, after which he received $250 per week with a six month option. This option allowed M–G–M to either renew or cancel the contract twice a year.

– Hugh Martin & Ralph Blane wrote a romantic ballad for the movie titled "I Know You By Heart". An orchestral arrangement of the song is in the final movie, but a vocal version by Tommy was deleted. However, the movie's soundtrack album from M–G–M includes Tommy's version.

– Hugh Martin and Ralph Blane went on to compose the music and lyrics for a number of other M–G–M musicals including *Broadway Rhythm, Meet Me in St. Louis,* and *Ziegfeld Follies*. Their most popular song was the Christmas carol "Have Yourself a Merry Little Christmas". Both men were inducted into the Songwriters Hall of Fame in 1983.

– Although Arthur Freed's reputation as a producer of successful movie musicals was well established before *Best Foot Forward*, his most memorable musicals followed. These included *Meet Me in St. Louis*, *Ziegfeld Follies*, *Easter Parade*, *Annie Get Your Gun*, *Show Boat*, *An American in Paris*, *Singin' in the Rain*, *Brigadoon*, and *Gigi*.

– Even though most of the cast of *Best Foot Forward* sang their own songs, three were dubbed. Gloria Grafton dubbed the songs for Lucille Ball, Louanne Hogan* dubbed Virginia Weidler, and Ralph Blane dubbed the songs for Jack Jordan. (*Some sources say Jeanne Darrell.)

– Virginia Weidler, who played Tommy's girlfriend in the movie, had played Katharine Hepburn's younger sister in *The Philadelphia Story* (1940) and been in over 40 other films. Although she was only 16 when she made *Best Foot Forward*, it was the last feature film she would ever be in.

– The artwork for the *Best Foot Forward* movie posters was drawn by the legendary caricaturist Al Hirschfeld.

– The stand–in for Tommy Dix (the person used to set up shots before a scene is actually filmed) was the same person used by Mickey Rooney.

– In 1943 Hollywood's major companies released 289 feature–length films. Only 10 of them were filmed in color. Four of those ten (including *Best Foot Forward*) were from M–G–M.

– The final cost of making *Best Foot Forward* was $1,125,502, and its box office gross receipts were $2,704,000. *Girl Crazy*, for comparison, cost $1,410,850 and had box office receipts of $3,771,000.

Kenny Bowers, Lucille Ball, and Tommy Dix
Relaxing between shots while filming *Best Foot Forward*

PHOTOFEST

Best Foot Forward had its World Premiere at the Astor Theatre in New York City on June 29, 1943, where it played for eleven weeks. It then moved over to the Loew's Theatres where it continued playing until its national release on October 8, 1943. *The New York Times* called the movie, *" . . . a rollicking musical film which pops with hilarious situations, sparkling dialogue and the fresh spirit of youth."* The review went on to say that, *"Tommy Dix is slightly over–pretty but very amusingly distraught as the hapless hero . . ."* Although the Mickey Rooney—Judy Garland musical comedy *Girl Crazy* would make more money for M–G–M that year, *Best Foot Forward* was a solid hit for the studio.

Tommy had received his military draft notice while he was making *Best Foot Forward,* but M–G–M obtained a 6–month deferment for him so he could complete the picture. This gave him time, after *Best Foot Forward* was completed, to perform with other entertainers for servicemen preparing to go overseas, like those in the newly activated Seventh Armored Division that was training in California.

> **Trivia:**
> – After the release of *Best Foot Forward*, Tommy Dix 'Fan Clubs' popped up around the country publishing a newsletter titled *The Winsocki Kid*.
> – The December 22, 1943, issue of *The Film Daily* published the results of an annual survey of press and radio critics and reviewers to determine the five best movie performers, directors and writers of the year. Under "Best Performances by Juvenile Actors" the winners were Mickey Rooney, Donald O'Conner, Roddy McDowall, Jack Jenkins & Tommy Dix.
> – In their September 1944 issue, the popular fan magazine *Modern Screen* published a two–page article about Tommy titled "Terrible Tommy".

Three young gentlemen on a date – with one glamour girl!

Black & White production stills from *Best Foot Forward*

44

Lucille Ball, Tommy Dix, and Virginia Weidler
Publicity photo for *Best Foot Forward* **(1943)**

LIVING IN 'TINSEL TOWN':

Tommy quickly discovered that everything was different in California — the attitude of the people, the climate, the scenery . . . everything — and he embraced the new lifestyle. When he reached Los Angeles he bought a used 1931 Model A Ford and his good friend Nancy Walker taught him to drive. He went out on dates with Virginia Weidler, the 16–year–old screen veteran who was playing his girlfriend in *Best Foot Forward*. (These 'dates' were arranged by the M–G–M Publicity Department who made sure they were covered by the press.) He associated with such actors as Laird Cregar who nicknamed Tommy "Carmine Lips".

> **Trivia:**
> — Laird Cregar was a cultivated, rather heavyset actor who would go on to
>   star in such thrillers as *The Lodger* (1944) and *Hangover Square* (1945).

Tommy also started going to the Beverly Hills Athletic Club where he enjoyed playing four–wall handball. One day, while watching some players on one of the courts, Tommy was asked if he would join them because they needed a fourth. One of the players was the comedian Phil Silvers; one was the songwriter Harry Akst; and the third was introduced as Ben Siegel. Tommy agreed, but while they were playing Tommy kept being blocked by Ben Siegel. It's illegal to block (hinder) someone from hitting the ball, and it seemed to Tommy that Siegel was blocking him intentionally. Not wanting to call "hinders" over and over, Tommy kept playing until his irritation overcame him.

"I'm not going to continue playing if you're going to keep blocking me," Tommy protested. In a flash both Phil Silvers and Harry Akst grabbed Tommy and escorted him out of the enclosed court. "Don't you know who that man is," Phil Silvers whispered.

"I don't give a damn who he is," Tommy declared, "if he can't play fair I don't want to play with him!"

"He's Bugsy Siegel," Phil Silvers said through clenched teeth, "the guy who runs *Murder, Incorporated*!"

Tommy didn't know that the man he was playing against, Benjamin 'Bugsy' Siegel, was one of the most notorious and feared gangsters on the West Coast. If he had known he might not have been so forthright and emphatic. But the righteousness of youth overcame whatever fear he might have had and he repeated, "I don't care who he is, I don't like people who don't play fair!"

Bugsy Siegel couldn't help overhearing Tommy's outburst. He came over to Tommy and said rather apologetically, "I'm sorry I kept blocking you. Come on back in and lets play."

Surprisingly, that first meeting matured into something like a friendship between Bugsy and Tommy. They often met for a game of handball, and Tommy was invited over to Bugsy's home on a number of occasions. But when Tommy's mother learned that Bugsy had offered to get Tommy parts in any movie he wanted, she put her foot down and gave Tommy some valuable advice.

"Be friends with him if you want," she told Tommy, "but *never* take anything from him. Always remember, '*He who rides a tiger can never dismount*'." Tommy took her advice and never accepted anything from Bugsy Siegel.

> **Trivia:**
> – Bugsy Siegel was assassinated on June 20, 1947, while he was reading a
>   newspaper at his girlfriend's home. The crime was never solved.

MOVIE PALACE REVUES:

Most of the large, ornate movie palaces in major cities around the country, including the five 'Wonder Theatres' built by the Loew's Theatre chain in and around New York City, presented an elaborate live revue before dimming their lights and showing a first–run feature film. These popular vaudeville shows were a mixture of singers, dancers, and variety acts accompanied by a large orchestra or well–known band. After his stint in Hollywood, Tommy would go on to become a headline act in many of the revues put on in these beautiful movie theaters. Singing was all that Tommy ever wanted to do, and he never again actively pursued a career in acting even though he had signed a movie contract with M–G–M.

Mickey Rooney, Jackie Moran, and Tommy Dix
PHOTOFEST
A production still from *Andy Hardy's Blonde Trouble* (filmed in 1943)

Chapter 5

MILITARY SERVICE

After *Best Foot Forward* finished filming at the end of March, M–G–M signed Tommy Dix to a contract that gave him a salary of $250 a week with a six–month option. The option allowed the studio to review the contract twice a year giving them the power to either renew or cancel it. Every time they chose to renew the contract Tommy would get an additional $50 per week.

Even when M–G–M didn't require his presence, Tommy kept very busy. On April 2nd he took and easily passed the pre–qualifying test for the Army Specialized Training Program. He entertained troops at venues like The Hollywood Canteen and, on June 12th, the training camp of the Seventh Armored Division. On June 29th he attended the world premiere of *Best Foot Forward* in New York City. At the beginning of August Tommy went to the campus of the University of Nevada in Reno to film some scenes for *Andy Hardy's Blonde Trouble*. (While there he remembers attending a dinner where he sat next to Herbert Marshall, one of the veteran featured players in the movie, and being impressed by Marshall's sophistication and knowledge.)

Tommy Entertains the Troops at The Hollywood Canteen (1943)

By late August Tommy was back in New York City appearing at Loew's State Theatre to help them celebrate their 22nd anniversary. He made a lasting impression on the audience when he sang the songs "Great Day", "Old Man River", and "Buckle Down, Winsocki". He also made a lasting impression on the show's Master of Ceremonies, Ed Sullivan. While appearing on the stage at Loew's Tommy had the unique experience of seeing his name in lights on both sides of Broadway. His name was on the marquee of the Astor Theatre at 1531 Broadway advertising the movie *Best Foot Forward*; and his name was on the marquee of the Loew's State Theatre across the street at 1540 Broadway advertising his appearance on their stage.

Before Tommy joined the army he went to the William Morris Agency and asked them to intervene for him with M–G–M. He had been told that M–G–M would not be paying him while he was in the army despite his contract, even though they made exceptions for stars like Mickey Rooney, and that as a private in the army he would be making only $21 a month. His mother had little means of support and Tommy was worried she wouldn't have enough money to live on. He requested that M–G–M provide her with a small monthly stipend that he would pay back after his tour in the army was over. M–G–M denied his request, and he had to make other arrangements for his mother.

This would not be the last time Tommy butted heads with the powers–that–be at M–G–M, or discover that his agents at the William Morris Agency were not too enthusiastic about challenging M–G–M's decisions concerning Tommy's career. Tommy soon discovered that in Hollywood he was merely a 'human property' that the studio felt free to manipulate for their convenience.

Finally, on September 10th, Tommy officially joined the army. The following day, when the officer in charge found out who Tommy was, he was sent to participate in a radio program called "It's Maritime" for the U.S. Maritime Service Training Station.

THE "ARMY SPECIALIZED TRAINING PROGRAM":

In the spring of 1943 a new army program called the "Army Specialized Training Program" (ASTP) went into full operation around the country. It was set–up to identify, train, and educate academically–talented enlisted men. After basic training the army would provide those accepted into the program with a four–year college education in either the sciences, mathematics, medicine, engineering, or linguistics, followed by additional Army training and a commission. They would then be assigned where needed until the war ended.

Sometime during the filming of *Best Foot Forward* Tommy heard about the army program and felt that if he could pass the tests and get accepted into the program he would be able to finally receive the college education he had always wanted. In April

Tommy easily passed the army's tests and was classified A–12, the military's designation for high school students who, by pre–induction tests, had established their eligibility for the ASTP.

Trivia:
– Two tests were used by the army to identify people for the ASTP: the "Army General Classification Test" (AGCT) that tested general learning ability, and the "General Classification Test" (GCT) that measured verbal aptitude. At first a minimum score of 110 was required for acceptance into the program (equivalent to an IQ score of 108), but the minimum score was eventually raised to 115 (equivalent to an IQ score of 112). (The conversion of AGCT scores to equivalent IQ scores can be found in the book *Essentials of Psychology* by Donald M. Johnson.)
– Through the ASTP over 140,000 servicemen were enrolled in college courses before the program was terminated.

Pvt. Thomas P. Navard (Tommy Dix)

BASIC TRAINING:

Entering the army as a Private under his real name, Thomas P. Navard, Tommy left the glamour of Show Business and began his required basic training at Fort Benning, Georgia.

Tommy's army Basic Training lasted from October 25, 1943, to February 5, 1944. With the others in his regiment (Fifth Company, Fifth Training Regiment, Army Specialized Training Program) he lived in a tarpaper barracks heated with a wood stove, and learned such things as how to shoot the Browning 1919 air–cooled machine gun and just how deadly mustard gas could be.

It was a full schedule of drilling, exercises, marches, and lectures. Periodically he and the others in the ASTP program had to take additional written exams. If someone failed one of these exams they were immediately removed from the program and reassigned to another regiment.

Very few people knew that Thomas P. Navard was really Tommy Dix, the star of the new M–G–M musical *Best Foot Forward*, and Tommy went out of his way to keep the other men in his regiment from finding out. He wanted to be just one of the guys, and he worked hard to become the best soldier he could be.

First Sergeant Sidney B. Smith and Pvt. Thomas P. Navard
Basic Training Center, Fort Benning, Georgia

One day during a routine exercise on a steep, narrow path, Tommy fell over a cliff and sustained a number of serious internal injuries. Not wanting to appear weak, he didn't tell anyone about the injuries until they were just too painful to endure. Although the doctors at Ft. Benning quickly identified and took care of Tommy's injuries, he developed a persistent case of diarrhea and began losing weight. Nothing he did or ate seemed to help, but Tommy continued on and never complained.

One person who did discover Tommy's real identity was Vernon Noah, a chaplain on the Army Post who was also a voice–teacher and director of the Highlands United Methodist Church choir in Birmingham, Alabama. He asked Tommy if he would consider performing at the church if the chaplain could get him a weekend pass. Like everyone else going through basic training, Tommy would do almost anything for a weekend pass and he quickly agreed.

Trivia:
– Birmingham, Alabama, is just a three–hour drive from Fort Benning.
– In 1996 a musical about three World War II privates who were part of the Army's Specialized Training Program opened off–Broadway. Written by Raymond Fox, *Take It Easy* ran for 103 performances.

SINGING IN BIRMINGHAM:

News that Tommy Dix, the star of *Best Foot Forward*, was going to appear at the church in Birmingham, Alabama, somehow got out, and hours before he arrived the church began filling up with teenagers who had seen the movie. *Best Foot Forward* had recently been released in Birmingham theaters, and so many of Tommy's new fans filled the church that many members of the congregation couldn't get in.

One member of the church who did get in was W.W. "Foots" Clements, a politically influential executive of the Dr. Pepper soft drink company. After Tommy finished singing and signing autographs, Mr. Clements introduced himself and told Tommy he was also the chairman of the Jefferson County War Bond Drive. He pointed out that Tommy could be quite valuable to the war effort if he used his talents and popularity to raise money selling War Bonds.

When Tommy's basic training ended on February 5th, 1944, he took advantage of a furlough his regiment had been given to make some personal appearances on behalf of the War Bond Drive with amazing results. At the Ansley High School in Birmingham, for example, Tommy sold $48,000 in bonds. Mr. Clements was now convinced that Tommy Dix was the celebrity he needed to promote the sale of War Bonds in his area of Alabama, but Tommy still wanted to go to college under the Army's Specialized Training Program.

Then, on February 18th, the War Department suddenly and unexpectedly announced that the ASTP was being disbanded due to the urgent need for additional manpower in Europe, and 110,000 ASTP students were abruptly recalled from colleges to active duty. Tommy's involvement in the ASTP was suddenly over and he learned that his regiment was being deployed overseas. Mr. Clements, meanwhile, was still working hard to convince Tommy that Alabama was where he was really needed, and after a great deal of thought Tommy accepted his offer to help sell War Bonds.

After Tommy agreed, it didn't take long for Mr. Clements to pull some strings and get Tommy transferred from his regiment to the 2nd Training Regiment at Fort McClellan in Anniston, Alabama. Using Fort McClellan as his base, Tommy traveled around central Alabama drawing large crowds at rallies and speaking at schools. He eventually sold over $3 million worth of War Bonds.

Pvt. Thomas P. Navard (1944)
After completing his Army Basic Training

Trivia:
– Over the course of the war 85 million Americans purchased War Bonds totaling approximately $185.7 billion.

TOMMY FALLS IN LOVE:

One of the venues where Tommy held rallies to sell bonds was the Alabama Theatre in Birmingham. During one rally a young girl was sent up to the stage by her

Margaret Ann Grayson (1946)
Her Brooke Hill School graduation photo

father to purchase a $1,000 War Bond. She was a striking, blonde, blue–eyed teenager who was attending the Brooke Hill School, a college preparatory school for girls. Tommy saw her and immediately knew she was someone he had to meet.

The young girl was Margaret Ann 'Maggie' Grayson, the daughter of a wealthy Birmingham building contractor and lumberyard owner. Introduced to each other by Stanley Mallotte, the organist at the rally, Tommy and Maggie started dating and they quickly fell in love. After he left the army and returned to Show Business, Tommy returned to Birmingham frequently to visit Maggie until she graduated from school in 1946 and they were able to marry.

Whether it was fate or destiny is unclear, but Tommy has had a curious connection to Birmingham, Alabama, throughout his life. His father was from Birmingham; Hugh Martin, one of the composers for *Best Foot Forward*, was from Birmingham; and now he had fallen in love with a girl from Birmingham. Within a few years his bond with the city would grow even stronger when he became one of its prominent citizens.

> **Trivia:**
> – In the school's 1946 yearbook it was noted that Maggie was the 1945–46 Vice–President of the Student Council, and that, *"On the greyest of Monday mornings, in she breezes, cheerful and smiling, and making everyone happy just by her own sweet manner."*

'Major' Bowes invited Pvt. Tommy Dix to perform on his radio show on May 11, 1944

MEDICAL DISCHARGE:

All during the time Tommy was raising money selling war bonds, the incessant diarrhea that had plagued him since basic training continued. Finally, after his weight had dropped from 130 to 96 pounds, he was hospitalized. While being questioned about his past medical history Tommy admitted to the doctor that he had been diagnosed with Celiac Disease when he was a child but never mentioned it to the army recruiter. The doctor said that the injuries Tommy had incurred during basic training had apparently caused his Celiac Disease to flare up, and once again he was unable to properly digest fats and wheat protein (gluten). Since he would need to adhere to a strict diet that the army could not provide, the doctor said that Tommy would have to be discharged as soon as they could get him back to his normal weight.

In the spring of 1944 Tommy was transferred to the Battey General Hospital near Rome, Georgia, to recuperate. Opened in March of 1943, the Battey General Hospital was a vast compound constructed on 160 acres specifically for sick, wounded, and disabled World War II servicemen.

By the summer of 1944 Tommy had regained his normal weight. Although his physical condition was still listed as 'Poor', on July 21st he received an Honorable Discharge from the army and $150.80. Once again, he was a civilian.

"Ach! Goebbels, ve are finished!"

From the LSU campus paper *The Reveille* (1944)

Chapter 6

PERFORMING ON THE ROAD

TOMMY RETURNS TO SHOW BUSINESS:

At this time most nightclubs, hotels, and other venues tended to prefer one talent agency over another when they needed musicians and performers for their shows. Agencies would often compete against each other to offer the best deal to a top venue, and it was not unusual for a venue to suddenly switch to another agency. This is what happened at the Copley–Plaza Hotel's Oval Room in Boston shortly before Tommy Dix was discharged from the army.

The two largest talent agencies in the early 1940s were MCA (Music Corporation of America) and the William Morris Agency. For the past year and a half the Oval Room had been booked almost exclusively by MCA. However, when Chauncey Depew Steele, the Room's general manager, left in June, his successor chose the William Morris Agency to supply most of their needed talent.

When Tommy was discharged from the army on July 21st and suddenly available again, M–G–M wanted him back in Hollywood. Tommy ignored their request and allowed his agent at the William Morris Agency to book him into the Palmer House Hotel's Empire Room and the Agency's newly acquired Oval Room at the Copley–Plaza in Boston. It was almost as though Tommy had never been away from Show Business.

After his August engagement in Boston was over, Tommy returned to New York City where he was soon contacted by Ed Sullivan. In addition to writing a column for the New York Daily News, Ed worked as an emcee for the vaudeville revues at the Loew's State Theatre on Broadway. Tommy's singing talent had impressed Ed when they had met the previous year, and he asked Tommy if he would sing in the Loew's State Theater's revue to mark his return to Show Business. Tommy accepted and, on September 7, 1944, Ed Sullivan introduced the "Private with the Sergeant's voice" from the stage of the prestigious Loew's State Theatre, and Tommy's powerful baritone voice once again filled the auditorium. After that success, M–G–M decided to let Tommy continue performing in live shows for the time being.

Through the William Morris Talent Agency Tommy immediately began getting bookings at the most famous nightclubs and theatres around the country. Among these were: the Persian Room at the Plaza Hotel in New York City; The Empire Room at the Palmer House in Chicago; the Golden Gate Theatre in San Francisco; the Ritz–Carlton Hotel in Boston; the Mayflower Hotel in Washington, DC; the Roosevelt Hotel's Blue

60

Room in New Orleans; the Earle Theatre in Philadelphia; the Latin Quarter nightclub in New York City; and the legendary Last Frontier Hotel in Las Vegas (to name but a few). For the rest of the 1940s Tommy was in constant demand as a headline act.

He was also welcomed back by his peers. On both June 3rd, 1945, and January 19th, 1947, Tommy was the guest of honor at a Leon & Eddie's 'Celebrity Party'. Leon & Eddie's was a popular New York City nightclub, and their Sunday night 'Celebrity Parties' attracted many of the city's most famous celebrities and entertainers. Among other performers who were honored at these parties were Bob Hope, Red Skelton, and Milton Berle.

For six years Tommy crisscrossed the nation performing in nightclubs, vaudeville shows, supper clubs, country clubs, and at special events. He was also a frequent guest on radio shows like Major Bowes' *The Shower of Stars* where he performed with the Morton Gould Orchestra, and *The Jerry Lawrence Show* on WMCA in New York City.

THE PALMER HOUSE:

One venue that Tommy was invited back to repeatedly, for as long as three months at a time, was the Empire Room at the Palmer House Hotel in Chicago. The

The EMPIRE ROOM of the PALMER HOUSE in CHICAGO

A vintage postcard showing The Empire Room in the late 1940s

entertainment at the Empire Room was ruled over by Merriell Abbott who produced the shows and provided the "Abbott Dancers" for the show's chorus line from a dance school she ran. When she first saw Tommy, shortly after he had returned to Show Business, she asked him why he was going to sing "The Lord's Prayer" during his set. She wondered whether it was appropriate to sing a religious song in a nightclub where drinks were being served. When Tommy explained that he wanted to sing it for "the boys overseas", she sheepishly agreed to let him do it. Then on opening night when he appeared wearing his usual sport coat, slacks and tie, Merriell asked him where his tuxedo was. When he explained that he didn't own a tuxedo, she insisted that the next day he find a tailor and have one made. "No one performs at The Palmer House without a tuxedo," she insisted.

Tommy went out that night and drew loud applause for his renditions of "Old Man River", and "Buckle Down, Winsocki". But toward the end of his act, when he sang "The Lord's Prayer", everything came to a complete standstill. The song touched the hearts of the war–weary audience, and when the last note faded away they broke into a thunderous standing ovation stopping the show cold in its tracks. When Tommy left the stage Merriell was waiting for him and, with a tear in her eye, she said softly, "Forget what I said. Don't change a thing."

Trivia:
– Merriell Abbott was a choreographer, guardian, and ever–watchful mother to her young dancers. She decided whom they could date (no orchestra players, please) and even had them weigh–in every Thursday morning to make sure their figures remained trim.
– In 1944 a dinner at the Palmer House's Empire Room cost $3.
– While performing in Chicago and other cities Tommy continued to entertain servicemen whenever he could. On October 6th, 1944, he received a *Certificate of Appreciation* from the Gardiner General Hospital in Chicago for providing "good wholesome entertainment for the patients and men."

SONG CHOICES:

Tommy never chose his songs from the pop hits on Billboard magazine's weekly charts. He preferred to sing memorable songs with beautiful lyrics. Along with venerable tunes like "Old Man River", hymns like "The Lord's Prayer", familiar arias, and standards from composers like George Gershwin, Oley Speaks, and Victor Herbert, Tommy's performances always included one or two numbers that almost no one else was singing. For instance, when the war was still being fought and Russia was America's ally, Tommy often sang "Song of the Plains" (the Red Army song "Polyushka Polye") — in Russian. He also sang such unusual pieces as "Song from the Rubáiyát of Omar Khayyám", "Myself When Young" (another song with lyrics based on the Rubáiyát), the Scottish ballad "Lord Randall", and the show tune "Lost in the Stars" that included the lyrics:

> *But I've been walking through the night, and the day*
> *Til my eyes get weary and my head turns grey*
> *And sometimes it seems maybe God's gone away*
> *Forgetting the promise that we've heard him say*
> *And we're lost out there in the stars.*

But each performance invariably concluded with Tommy's rousing rendition of "Buckle Down, Winsocki" from *Best Foot Forward*. It had become his signature song, and no one ever sang it better.

RESTRICTIONS ON MAKING RECORDS:

In 1945 M–G–M announced plans to establish its own record label. Consequently the studio told all the singers it had under contract, in no uncertain terms, that their studio contract prohibited them from making or renewing any recording contracts with other record labels. Along with Judy Garland and other M–G–M singers, Tommy Dix was affected by this ruling.

Unfortunately, during the rest of the 1940s M–G–M Records limited its releases to soundtrack albums from the studio's musical films, not new recordings from its artists, so Tommy was unable to make any commercial records. He did make a recording rather surreptitiously for Coronet Records in 1947 (COR–101), but to avoid an M–G–M lawsuit it was released "For Home Use Only" and could not be played on the radio. Not surprisingly, very few were sold.

Eventually M–G–M Records released the entire soundtrack from *Best Foot Forward* — including the ballad "I Know You By Heart" that had been recorded by Tommy but cut from the movie — on a 33rpm long–playing record (a recording that is still available on CD). But other than that record and his 1941 recording of "Buckle Down, Winsocki", no other commercial recordings by Tommy have ever been released.

MARRIAGE:

Despite his hectic schedule, Tommy continued to visit his girlfriend in Birmingham, Alabama, as often as he could, sometimes even overcoming his fear of flying and arriving by plane. Tommy's career was booming, and by early 1946 he was living in a large New York City apartment at #1 West 68th Street, overlooking Central Park.

Margaret Ann 'Maggie' Grayson & Tommy Dix (1946)

His schedule during the first half of 1946 gives some indication of how hectic Tommy's career had become (some dates are missing):

January 7th to February 8th: Performs at the Chez Paree nightclub in Chicago.

January 17th: Takes one night off from the Chez Paree to appear in an All–Star Revue at the Palmer House's Empire Room.

February 11th to February 20th: Performs in a revue at the Oriental Theatre in Chicago. He is described as "a local favorite".

February 22nd to February 28th: Performs at the Hilton Hotel's Boulevard Room Supper Club in Chicago.

March 15th: Appears in the *Cavalcade of Stars* held at Chicago Stadium for disabled American veterans. 20,000 people come to the show.

March 16th to March 23rd: Maggie, her brother, and her parents visit Tommy in New York City. All of the Graysons stay at the Commodore Hotel. Tommy and Maggie apply for a marriage license.

April 9th to April 11th: Tommy flies into Birmingham, AL, to visit Maggie. He gives her a diamond ring with birthstones (his and hers) flanking either side. They had designed the ring together when they became engaged the previous Christmas, although they don't formally announce their engagement until June 9th. Tommy performs at the Exchange Club.

April 12th to April 20h: Performs at the Beverly Hills Country Club in Newport, KY (a famous nightclub/casino owned by the crime syndicate in Cleveland).

May 8th: Sings at the *Cavalcade of Stars* for disabled veterans in Buffalo, NY.

May 13th to May 22nd: Visits Maggie in Birmingham, AL.

May 17th to May 24th: Performs in a revue with Eddie Bracken at various theaters including the Earle Theatre in Philadelphia, the Metropolitan Theatre in Pittsburg, and the State Theater in Hartford, CT, among others.

May 27th: Heads a program of variety acts at the RKO Proctor Theatre in Mount Vernon, NY.

May 29th: Tommy flies to Birmingham, AL, to appear with Hugh Martin at the annual meeting of the Birmingham–Southern College Alumni Association. Tommy sings Hugh Martin's song "Buckle Down, Winsocki" while Martin accompanies him on the piano. Tommy then escorts Maggie to her school formal sponsored by Alpha Delta Psi.

June 5th to June 11th: Performs at the Olympia Theatre in Miami, FL.

June 12th to June 17th: Appears at the Kitty Davis Airliner nightclub in Miami.

Trivia:

– In March Maggie wrote to Marie Pellegrini, the president of the 'national' Tommy Dix Fan Club in New York City, asking if she could start a chapter of the Fan Club in Birmingham, AL. (Maggie didn't identify who she was or her connection to Tommy.) Marie replied that Maggie could only start an 'official' chapter if she could get 30 to 35 other fans to join. Maggie decided to just send in her dollar membership fee for which she received a membership card and a photo of Tommy.

On June 29, 1946, Thomas Paine Dix Navard (Tommy Dix) and Margaret Ann Grayson were married at the First Baptist Church in Birmingham, Alabama. It was an exquisite wedding with Maggie dressed in a custom–designed gown from New York City of ivory slipper satin draped in rose point lace. Her eight bridesmaids were dressed in white net with romantic

THIS IS TO CERTIFY THAT

Margaret Ann Grayson

is a member of the

Tommy Dix Fan Club

Marie Pellegrini
President

necklines outlined in rows of net puffing, fitted bodices, and bouffant skirts. Each wore a red rose in her hair. Corporal William Redfield of New York City was Tommy's best man.

The following day, even as scores of congratulatory telegrams continued to pour in from across the country, Maggie and Tommy left for their honeymoon on Miami Beach. Staying at the beautiful Cadillac Hotel, an art deco gem that had opened in 1940, the couple enjoyed the warm sun and pleasant ocean breezes of Miami Beach — but only for a short time.

Even while honeymooning there was no pause in Tommy's career, and shortly after they arrived on Miami Beach Tommy accepted an invitation to perform again at the nearby *Kitty Davis Airliner* nightclub. Headlining a show that included Josephine Delmar (the 'Puerto Rican Bombshell'), Lou Saxon ('Broadway's Favorite Raconteur'), two bands, and an all–star cast, Tommy once again was delighting an audience with renditions of "Great Day" (a Negro folk song), "Roger Young" (a World War II ballad), and "Because" (a romantic French ballad translated into English by Edward Teschemacher).

Shortly after his wedding, M–G–M contacted Tommy and said they finally had another picture for him and they wanted him back in Hollywood. Tommy and Maggie packed up, moved to California's San Fernando Valley, and bought a house. But when Tommy showed up for work at the M–G–M lot he was told his part had been given to someone else and, to add insult to injury, the studio had dropped the option on his contract. Tommy has always felt that this was how M–G–M got their revenge on him for not immediately reporting back to the studio when he was discharged from the army.

Despite this small setback, Tommy and Maggie were happy and could afford to live quite comfortably on the income from his live appearances. But though the family moved back to New York City so they could be together more often, the frequent separations caused by Tommy's non–stop schedule began to put a strain on his marriage. Maggie and their son Grayson Henry (who was born on May 4th, 1947) meant so much to Tommy that he began thinking about retiring from the professional stage and taking up a "normal" life.

EDITH FELLOWS:

Tommy Dix & Edith Fellows at the Stork Club in NYC

Thoughts of retirement were put on temporary hold when Freddie Fields, an important theatrical agent with the Music Corporation of America, contacted Tommy and suggested that he team–up with Freddie's wife, Edith Fellows.

Edith had been a popular child actress during the 1930s and early 1940s, appearing in almost 50 movies – most notably with Bing Crosby in *Pennies From Heaven* (1936) and a series of four *Five Little Peppers* movies in 1939/1940. (For one movie in 1938 Columbia Pictures publicized her as "*your favorite cyclone in curls*".) She was a versatile actress and an accomplished singer with a beautiful soprano voice. Once she had outgrown juvenile roles she went on the road appearing in regional plays, vaudeville shows, and nightclubs with mixed success.

In 1946 Edith married Freddie Fields, and he eventually decided that teaming her with Tommy would be a good professional move for both of them. In October, 1948,

Edith Fellows

Tommy and Edith announced that they would become a team and they began preparing an act that combined light comedy with singing. Building the act for almost six months while Tommy continued to perform around the country, they finally opened at the Olympia Theatre in Miami at a benefit concert. Sid Piermont, the head of Loew's booking agency, was in the audience and he immediately offered to book them at the Capitol Theatres in Washington, DC, and New York City. A whirlwind of non–stop bookings at theaters and clubs around the country quickly followed, and the bookings continued in high gear until the middle of the following year when Tommy finally decided he had had enough.

A reviewer for the trade magazine *Billboard* gave this description of Tommy & Edith's act in 1950:

> **The two kids showed verve, freshness and a sense of showmanship indicative of their combined experience in various branches of showbiz. Basically Miss Fellows does the heavy comedy and Dix is the light comic, with both blending voices on singing duets. Team started off with a reverse gimmick doing a *Goodbye* for an opener. Then came *I Can Do Anything Better*, a hypoed version of *You're the Top*, winding up with a slightly satiric tho highly amusing and effective medley of *South Pacific* tunes. Basically, the Dix and Fellows forte is comedy. They proved it in various bits of business.**

Trivia:
- Edith Marilyn Fellows was born on May 20, 1923. She made her movie debut in 1929, and in the mid–1930s Columbia Pictures signed her to a seven–year contract — the first such deal offered to a child.
- As an adult Edith Fellows was only 4'10" tall.
- Edith's earnings were put in a trust when she was a child, and by 1939 her estate was estimated to be worth $150,000 (about $2.5 million in today's money). On her 21st birthday she went to claim her money and discovered that there was only $900 left in the trust. She never found out what happened to the rest of her money.
- A play about Edith Fellows as a child actress was written by Rudy Benz in 1979. Titled *Dreams Deferred*, the play opened at a small theatre in Los Angeles with Edith playing herself.
- Edith died on June 26, 2011.
- Edith's daughter, Kathy, is married to David Lander who played Squiggy on *Laverne & Shirley*, a popular TV show that ran from 1976 to 1983.

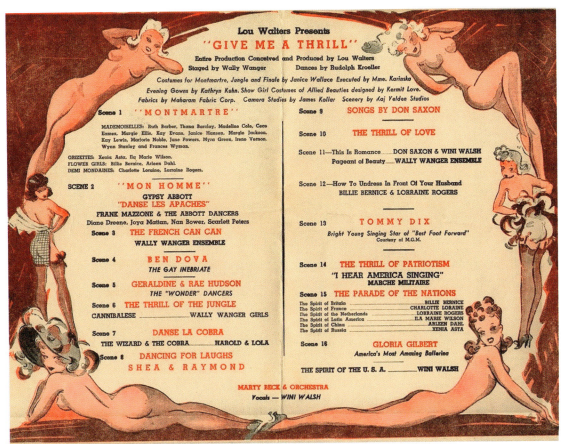

Tommy joined this revue at The Latin Quarter in May 1945

THE LATIN QUARTER:

New York City's *Latin Quarter* was a popular nightclub that Lou Walters opened in 1942 at the corner of 48th Street and Broadway. Modeled somewhat after *The Moulin Rouge* in Paris, the shows at *The Latin Quarter* featured elaborate settings and costumes, a chorus line of beautiful dancing girls, famous bands, and big–name acts from every area of Show Business. There were also branches of Walters' *Latin Quarter* nightclub in Boston, Miami Beach, and Chicago, and entertainers like Frank Sinatra, Dean Martin & Jerry Lewis, Jack Benny, Milton Berle, and Tony Bennett regularly performed at these clubs intermingled with waves of high–kicking chorus girls.

After Tommy returned to Show Business in 1944, many of his professional engagements were at the New York City's *Latin Quarter* and its branches. Over time Lou Walters and Tommy became close friends, and when Tommy and Edith Fellows formed their act they were quickly booked into Lou Walters' clubs.

But Tommy's growing disenchantment with the world of entertainment and the adverse effects of his hectic schedule had finally taken their toll, and at the end of July, 1950, while performing at the *Latin Quarter* in New York City, Tommy suddenly announced his retirement from Show Business. Although he and Edith were already booked to play the Flamingo Hotel in Las Vegas, the Coconut Grove in Los Angeles, the Palmer House in Chicago, and the Roxy Theatre in New York City (bookings that would have brought them $19,900), Tommy realized that continually being on the road had become critically detrimental to his relationship with his family. He decided that he needed to focus on his wife and child, not on his Show Business career. While still one of the most popular nightclub acts in the country, Tommy Dix called it quits.

> **Trivia:**
> – Lou Walters was the father of the journalist Barbara Walters.
> – The *Latin Quarter's* prices were very modest — a two–dollar minimum and an average dinner tab of eight dollars a person which could include shrimp cocktail, salad, steak, and dessert.
> – The productions at the *Latin Quarter* were changed twice a year, and each cost between $75,000 and $80,000.

Chapter 6

LIFE AFTER SHOW BUSINESS

Flanked by long parallel mountain ridges running northeast to southwest, Birmingham, Alabama, is nestled in the Jones Valley near the center of the state. Nicknamed 'The Magic City', it is probably better known as 'The Pittsburgh of the South' because of its iron and steel production. It is also one of the two main railroad hubs in the Deep South (the other being Atlanta). By the middle of the 20th Century the city had become an important center for banking, telecommunications, transportation, electrical power transmission, medical care, college education, and insurance.

In 1950 the population of Birmingham was just over 325,000 (60% white, 40% black), making it the largest city in the state and the 34th largest in the United States. Racial segregation was still widely practiced in Birmingham and throughout Alabama during the early 1950s, but the beginning of the end came in 1954 when the U.S. Supreme Court ruled against segregated schools. Even so, Birmingham became one of the centers of the Civil Rights struggle during the late '50s and early '60s until the U.S. Congress passed the Civil Rights Act of 1964 and the Voting Rights Act of 1965.

EMBRACING BIRMINGHAM:

Having said "good–bye" to Show Business, Tommy accepted a position at his father–in–law's lumberyard, and by the fall of 1950 he and his family had moved to Birmingham. With the move came an abrupt decrease in his income from up to $3,000 per week to $200 per month plus room and board. But at last Tommy could come home to his family every night, and he embraced the change.

Tommy became the Associate Minister of Music at a local Baptist Church, and using the G.I. Bill he went back to school and earned an Associate Degree in Architectural Engineering with a minor in Business Law. But there were still opportunities to perform and he couldn't resist taking advantage of them almost as soon as he arrived in the city.

THE CALL OF THE STAGE:

In 1950 James Hatcher, an instructor in speech at the University of Alabama, brought together a group of university alumni who were interested in forming a community theater in Birmingham. The group, made up mostly of volunteers, took the name *Town & Gown*. Using various venues around Birmingham, their first production,

Born Yesterday, opened at the Masonic Temple on December 7, 1950. It starred Peggy Lippe and Tommy Dix.

In 1955 the *Town & Gown* took up permanent residence in the historic Little Theater, which was renovated and renamed the Clark Memorial Theater, and at the beginning of the following year they presented their first musical, *Best Foot Forward*. The now famous composer, songwriter, and Alabama native, Hugh Martin, and his sister came in to help stage the production, and Tommy Dix was chosen to lead the cast.

While continuing to work at his day job, first in the lumberyard (where he had become a vice–president) and then as a builder of single–family homes, Tommy took part in almost every form of entertainment the city had to offer. He continued to work with the *Town & Gown* community theater; he was one of the organizers of the Birmingham Civic Ballet Association; he was the director of Birmingham's second annual *Christmas Festival at City Hall*; he sang in the summer concerts held at Woodrow Wilson Park; he produced and was the Master of Ceremonies for the annual *Music Under the Stars* concerts at Legion Field; and he was even the Master of Ceremonies at the Miss Alabama Pageant Finals held in 1954. Tommy was generous with his time and talent, but *only* if it filled a civic or charitable purpose.

In 1952 Tommy went to see the Western movie *High Noon*. As soon as he heard Tex Ritter sing the haunting ballad "Do Not Forsake Me" he was deeply moved and knew that he had to add the song to his music repertoire. Returning home he wasted no time writing a fan letter to Dimitri Tiomkin, the man who had written the theme song and conducted the soundtrack for *High Noon*. In the letter he expressed his desire to add the opening song to his music catalog. Quite unexpectedly Tiomkin not only wrote back but also sent Tommy his entire hand–written orchestration for the movie — a treasure that thrilled Tommy and one that he made use of often during his future concerts.

Trivia:
- On January 8, 1953, Tommy's second son was born. He was named Brittain Claude, but became known to almost everyone as 'Britt'. In 1965, when he was only 12, Britt unexpectedly and tragically died.
- The song "Do Not Forsake Me" from the movie *High Noon* was the first song from a non–musical film to win an Academy Award.
- In October 1974, Tommy returned to the *Town & Gown* Theater's stage to participate in a benefit performance in the new theater of the Birmingham Jefferson Civic Center. This gala 'Silver Anniversary Celebration' brought back to Birmingham many former *Town & Gown* stars.

Music Under The Stars

Legion Field
Birmingham, Alabama

May 18, 1954
8:00 P. M.

PROGRAM

TOMMY DIX, *Master of Ceremonies*

THE NATIONAL ANTHEM

Egmont Overture ....*Beethoven*
Tribute to Romberg ....*Arr. MacLean*
BIRMINGHAM SYMPHONY ORCHESTRA
Walter Moeck, Conducting

King Jesus Is A-Listening ....*Arr. Dawson*
Deep River...*Arr. Burleigh*
Mountains ....*Rasbach*
PARKER HIGH SCHOOL CHOIR
William S. Henry, Director

Artists' Life Waltz...*Strauss*
LEVINGE SCHOOL OF THE DANCE
Natalie Levinge Webb, Director

Come to the Fair ....*Martin*
MAYPOLE DANCERS
Pratt School, Mrs. Ruby Kelley, Director; Miss Sybil McKinley, Assistant
Minor School, Mrs. Willie Perry Rose, Director; Mrs. Bebe Brewer, Assistant
Jackson School, Mrs. LeNelle Evans, Director

Gypsy Airs ....*Sarasote*
BIRMINGHAM SYMPHONY ORCHESTRA
Herbert Levinson, Violin Soloist

Old Man River from *Showboat*...*Kern*
Stouthearted Men from *The New Moon* ....*Romberg*
The Lord's Prayer..*Malotte*
Tommy Dix

Euryanthe Overture ....*Weber*
BIRMINGHAM SYMPHONY ORCHESTRA

AFTER BIRMINGHAM:

In 1959, after 13 years of marriage, Tommy and his wife divorced and he sadly decided to leave Birmingham and seek his fortune elsewhere. His first move was to Maryland where he became Director of Marketing and Sales for Panitz Bros. & Company who were developing the planned community of Joppatowne near the Chesapeake Bay.

Featuring everything from garden apartments, town houses, and a wide variety of single–family homes, to schools, churches, and commercial areas, Joppatowne became Tommy's new home for the next four years. He improved the models, refined and enhanced Joppatowne's brochures and advertisements, and settled a contentious dispute with the electric utility company that gave them a prized "Electric City" designation. He also wrote and narrated a 15–minute promotional film about Joppatowne that was played continuously at the Visitors' Center.

Although his work with Panitz Bros. was very successful, winning him an award from *American Builder* magazine for achieving almost $10,000,000 worth of sales in one year, he continued to sing

One of the models available at Joppatowne.
Joppatowne home prices in 1960 ranged from $8,990 to $12,990

and encourage others to sing. To this end he formed the *Joppatowne Choral Society* and opened it up to anyone interested in singing. They performed at a number of civic events.

In 1964 Tommy left Joppatowne and went to Sarasota, Florida, where he directed residential building for Rutenberg Homes. From there Tommy moved to the rapidly expanding southeastern coast of Florida where condominium complexes and subdivisions were being developed on a large scale. These "planned recreational communities", that combined ownership with care–free living, attracted Tommy and he started specializing in real estate marketing. Within a few years he had become the project manager for the state's two largest subdivisions; played a leading role in the marketing and sales of some

Tommy receives an award from *American Builder* magazine (early 1960s)

of southeastern Florida's most important developments; and innovated a number of marketing and design approaches that put him at the top of his field. In fact, if this book were a history of Florida real estate development in the latter half of the 20th Century, Tommy's achievements in that area would merit a lengthy and important section.

By 1981 Tommy and two partners formed their own company that offered support for developers on a 'fee plus participating' basis. This allowed them to share their competency in design, conception, management, financing, marketing, administration, training, research, etc., for much more money than they had made as employees of a single developer. Their list of clients soon included Domaine Delray, Wellington Royal Homes, the Evergreen Corporation, the Radice Corporation, and Ashland Oil to name but a few. Tommy also began making a methodical study of how stocks and bonds are bought, sold, and traded, a study that he continues to pursue to this day.

THE SOCIETY OF ATHENS:

In 1975 Tommy formed an intellectual discussion group at Palm–Aire, one of his resort–condominium projects in Pompano Beach. He named the discussion group *The Society of Athens* to reflect the spirit of the 'Golden Age of Greece' when the pursuit of truth and reflection upon abstract ideas were valued and encouraged. Growing out of his lifelong commitment to the study and understanding of science, philosophy, and religion, Tommy wanted to offer residents an outlet for their intellectual curiosity. He felt strongly that, *"For too long a glaring omission in retirement communities has been the lack of accommodation for the people who wish to remain intellectually viable."*

Meeting on the second and fourth Sundays of every month, with Tommy as the moderator, *The Society of Athens* sometimes drew over 100 people to their discussions. The topics ranged from "Love, Sex, and the New Society" to "What is Happiness?" According to the rules set–up by Tommy, members had to stick to universals rather than talking subjectively, and not lash out at the ideas of others. *"The raison d'être,"* he wrote, *"is to provide a forum for free and uninhibited philosophical discussion, on subjects vital to the human condition, for those who feel at home in an intellectually challenging environment, and to provide a place where one is apt to meet others of similar inclination."*

STILL SINGING:

Although Tommy had little time for outside activities when he was working in real estate, he did make time on a few occasions to share his singing talent. In the early 1980s Tommy was featured at the annual *Salute to America* summer concerts put on by the *Boca Raton Pops Orchestra*. According to the *Boca Raton News*, *"The audience was hypnotized by the deep, dulcet tones of the former movie star turned realtor."* The newspaper went on to say that, *"Dix sent chills down everyone's spines with his impeccable version of 'Old Man River'."* Tommy also found time in the mid–1980s to perform with the *Sunrise Musical Theatre* in Sunrise, FL., and the *Sunrise Symphonic Pops Orchestra.* But, as in Birmingham, he continued to perform only as an unpaid volunteer. "I love it too much to sell it," he said. Throughout his life Tommy has always been ready and willing to freely lend his talents for any civic or charitable cause.

RETIREMENT:

In 1986, when he was only 62, Tommy decided the time had come to retire. He had lived a full life up to that time, first as a very successful entertainer on stage, screen, radio and television, and then as a very successful real estate developer and entrepreneur — quite an accomplishment for someone who began life as a seriously ill young lad growing up in a poor section of New York City.

Tommy now lives contentedly in a beautiful area of Williamsburg, Virginia, surrounded by the books and art he collected over his lifetime. The preface to one of those books, *The Autobiography of Bertrand Russell*, might well have been written by Tommy himself:

Three passions, simple but overwhelmingly strong, have governed my life: the longing for love, the search for knowledge, and unbearable pity for the suffering of mankind. These passions, like great winds, have blown me hither and thither, in a wayward course, over a deep ocean of anguish, reaching to the very verge of despair.

I have sought love, first, because it brings ecstasy — ecstasy so great that I would often have sacrificed all the rest of life for a few hours of this joy. I have sought it, next, because it relieves loneliness — that terrible loneliness in which one shivering consciousness looks over the rim of the world into the cold unfathomable lifeless abyss. I have sought it, finally, because in the union of love I have seen, in a mystic miniature, the prefiguring vision of the heaven that the saints and poets have imagined. This is what I sought, and though it might seem too good for human life, this is what — at last — I have found.

With equal passion I have sought knowledge. I have wished to understand the hearts of men. I have wished to know why the stars shine. And I have tried to apprehend the Pythagorean power by which number holds sway above the flux. A little of this, but not much, I have achieved.

Love and knowledge, so far as they were possible, led upward toward the heavens. But always pity brought me to earth. Echoes of cries of pain reverberate in my heart. Children in famine, victims tortured by oppressors, helpless old people a hated burden to their sons, and the whole world of loneliness, poverty, and pain make a mockery of what human life should be. I long to alleviate the evil, but I cannot, and I too suffer.

This has been my life. I have found it worth living, and would gladly live it again if the chance were offered me.

BIBLIOGRAPHY

In addition to consulting many newspapers, magazines, and trade journals from the 1920s–1980s, I used the following books for my research into the life and times of Tommy Dix.

Allyson, June. *June Allyson*. New York: G.P. Putnam's Sons, 1982.

Barrymore, Ethel. *Memories: An Autobiography*. New York: Harper & Brothers, 1955.

Bingen, Steven, with Stephen X. Sylvester and Michael Troyan. *M–G–M: Hollywood's Greatest Backlot*. Solana Beach, CA: Santa Monica Press, 2011.

Bordman, Gerald. *American Musical Theatre: A Chronicle*. New York: Oxford University Press, 1978.

Bordman, Gerald. *American Theatre: A Chronicle of Comedy and Drama, 1930–1969*. New York: Oxford University Press, 1996.

Brown, Gene. *Show Time: A Chronology of Broadway and the Theatre from Its Beginnings to the Present*. New York: Macmillan, 1997.

Dunning, John. *On the Air: The Encyclopedia of Old–Time Radio*. New York: Oxford University Press, 1998.

Dworkin, Susan. *Miss America, 1945: Bess Myerson's Own Story*. New York: Newmarket Press, 1987.

Eames, John Douglas. *The MGM Story: The Complete History of Fifty–Seven Roaring Years*. New York: Crown Publishers, 1975, revised 1982.

Fordin, Hugh. *M–G–M's Greatest Musicals: The Freed Unit*. New York: Da Capo Press. 1996. Originally published as *The World of Entertainment! Hollywood's Greatest Musicals.* New York: Doubleday, 1975.

Fricke, John. *Judy: A Legendary Film Career*. Philadelphia, PA: Running Press Book Publishers, 2010.

Green, Stanley. *Broadway Musicals: Show by Show*. Milwaukee, WI: Applause Theatre & Cinema Books, Hal Leonard Corporation, 1985. Sixth edition 2008.

Green, Stanley. *Hollywood Musicals: Year by Year*. Milwaukee, WI: Hal Leonard Corporation, 1990, revised 1999.

Hay, Peter. *MGM: When the Lion Roars*. Atlanta, GA: Turner Publishing, 1991.

Keefer, Louis E. *Scholars in Foxholes: The Story of the Army Specialized Training Program in World War II*. Jefferson, NC: McFarland & Company, Inc., 1988.

Martin, Hugh. *Hugh Martin: The Boy Next Door*. Encinitas, CA: Trolley Press, 2010.

Mordden, Ethan. *Beautiful Mornin': The Broadway Musical in the 1940s*. New York: Oxford University Press, 1999.

Phillips, Brent. *Charles Walters: The Director Who Made Hollywood Dance*. Lexington, KY: The University Press of Kentucky, 2014.

Rose, Frank. *The Agency: William Morris and the Hidden History of Show Business*. New York: HarperCollins Publishers, Inc., 1995.

St. John, Charles J. *God on the Bowery*. New York: Fleming H. Revell Company, 1940.

Steigman, Benjamin M. *Accent on Talent: New York's High School of Music and Art*. Detroit, MI: Wayne State University Press, 1964.

Walters, Barbara. *Audition: A Memoir*. New York: Alfred A. Knopf, 2008.

Yudkoff, Alvin. *Gene Kelly: A Life of Dance and Dreams*. New York: Back Stage Books, 1999.

82

BUCKLE DOWN, WINSOCKI
(Lyrics by Hugh Martin & Ralph Blane)

If you shout hooray for the Pennsylvania Dutchmen,
They will cover the groun'
for a number one down or a touch.
Ev'ry one is agreed that you have to concede
to the Dutchmen.
Shout hooray for the Pennsylvania Dutch.

If you shout hooray for the Pennsylvania Dutchmen,
Ev'ry team that they play will be carried away
with a crutch.
When they're out on the field
If they're wearing the shield of the Dutchmen,
Shout Hooray for the Pennsylvania Dutch — Hooray!

Buckle down Winsocki, buckle down!
You can win Winsocki if you knuckle down.
If you break their necks, if you make them wrecks,
You can break the hex, so buckle down.
Make 'em yell Winsocki, make 'em yell.
You can win, Winsocki, if you give 'em hell.
If you don't give in, take it on the chin,
You are bound to win, if you will only buckle down.

If you fight you'll chuckle at defeat.
If you fight your luck 'll not retreat.
Knuckle down Winsocki, knuckle down.
You can win, Winsocki, if you buckle down.
If you mow them down, if you go to town,
You can wear the crown if you will only buckle down.

THE MARCH OF DIMES
Dedicated to the Cause of the President's Birthday Ball
(Lyrics and Music by Tommy Dix)

Marching along singing a song
Of health and wealth and joy —
Marching away day after day
To help some girl or boy —

See them go by — onward they fly
Here come a million more —
To help our nation's girls and boys
Their health and strength restore.

Onward they go, faster the flow
Oh how your spirit climbs —
As you see them rolling on their way,
THE MARCH OF DIMES.

Helping, helping some girl or boy
To strength and health one day,
Helping them to know the joy of running off to play,
Helping each to ease his lot
Buying health for some poor tot —

Marching along, singing a song
Of health and wealth and joy —
Marching away day after day
To help some girl or boy —

Onward they go, faster the flow,
Oh how your spirit climbs —
As you see them rolling on their way,
THE MARCH OF DIMES.

(the first page of the sheet music can be seen on page 22)

84

Tommy Dix (1943)

GENESIS II
By Tommy Dix

When ancient eyes, now turned to dust,
Did first another's pain discern,
And lent compassion in return;
When man became, at last, a man,

When hearts, by faith, were warmed to trust,
And sparked brave fealty's flame to burn,
When life, for life, first showed concern,
       Then you
           and I
              and love
                  began.

ON CLOSING
By Tommy Dix

When that time of life arrives for gazing backward,
(As forward, there is little left to be)
There will loom no crowded myriad of memories,
Not for me.

No parade of deeds or places in my visions,
No accomplishments or conquests will I see,
But the bright and warming smiles upon the faces
Of the dear ones who I loved and who love me.

ACKNOWLEDGEMENTS

I wanted to take a moment to thank some of the people who made this book possible.

First I would like to thank Tommy Dix for his time, cooperation and friendship. I have truly enjoyed our many enlightening conversations and meetings, and I look forward to having many more in the future.

Next I would like to thank John Coles and Mark Tiedje who share my passion for old movies and movie history. It was because of our combined research that John initially found Tommy, and we all continue to share and enjoy everything we discover about the 'Golden Age' of Hollywood.

Saving the most important for last, I would like to acknowledge and thank my wife, Anne. Her tolerance of my eccentricities qualifies her for sainthood, and her editing skills are without equal. She has developed a deep affection for Tommy, and without her help and encouragement this book would probably still be languishing on my computer.

— *Ken Robichaux*

Tommy Dix and Ken Robichaux (2011)

Made in the USA
Lexington, KY
07 October 2015